Gift

Mary Coquillard —

Property of

Edna McElroy Coquillard
529 N. Park Ave.,
Winter Park — Florida

# THE
# SECOND TREASURY
## OF
# *Early American Homes*

# THE

# *Second Treasury of*

# EARLY AMERICAN

# HOMES

BY *Richard Pratt*

IN COLLABORATION WITH *Dorothy Pratt*

HAWTHORN BOOKS, INC.     PUBLISHERS

NEW YORK

*First Edition · October, 1954*

*To Joan*

# FOREWORD

ON the wall beside us is a single shelf the length of the room, filled from end to end with books that deal in one way or another with the early homes of this country. Standing at attention up there with their backs to us, the row is about fourteen feet long, and various to a degree. Large books, little ones, old, new and middle-aged. Some are learned and scholarly, fringed with footnotes and frowning with authority. One or two with the titles long since worn off their brown leather backs could have been held in the hands of colonial craftsmen. A few are truly monumental. And naturally a lot of them are delightful to look at. Certain favorites have been entertainment for us along with enlightenment, including one very good historical study that comes right out to proclaim itself "grimly didactic." And you may be sure there are many, many more than appear in this particular assembly. We imagine you might be able to turn up enough more titles to run right around the room from floor to ceiling. Indeed it would seem from simply the hundred titles contained on our single shelf that the subject of our heritage houses had by now been pretty well explored. Yet not until 1949 had any book ever portrayed these old houses as they really are in color. And there is no denying that when this finally happened just five years ago, in the case of the first *Treasury*, it caused that book to be received as something of a revelation; and also caused it to be quickly acquired by a record-making quarter-million readers. And now that the *Second Treasury* comes to reveal its own entirely new collection of early American homes in color, we can hope for it no better fate than befell its predecessor.

As with that first one, this book owes its being to the color-illustrated articles originally prepared for the Regional Series, running since 1946 in the *Ladies' Home Journal*. Without that inheritance it would have been impossible to publish this book at a price within the reach of the general public. So the significant fact which was stated in the first *Treasury* still stands, that only a magazine with millions of readers is able to undertake a project whose preparation costs alone would make a book of this kind prohibitive in price. Of course, no magazine with millions of readers is required to give copiously of its color space to a continuing series on a cultural level; and the fact that the *Journal* has been the only one ever to do so with our heritage houses makes the popularity of the series a tribute to the acumen of Bruce and Beatrice Blackmar Gould, the editors, whose idea it was to begin it and then to keep it going.

In a very real sense that series has created for our fine old houses a vast new public. How many people had ever been aware of what beauties were to be encountered, for instance, in New Castle, Delaware, or in Litchfield, Connecticut, until the choicest houses and interiors of those two still unspoiled towns were colorfully set before the *Journal's* tremendous audience? Or at Wilton, say, or Rock Hall, or the Ruggles house, or Pottsgrove, or the Pingree house in Salem?

Thus people in a truly widespread way in every part of the country have become acquainted with what must be the most historically handsome and certainly the most personally endearing of all our national resources. What have they seen? Well, since the outset of the *Journal* series, more than a hundred and fifty of these finest early homes have been featured inside and out, and many others shown, together with twenty-odd vintage towns and localities. Just about one half of the houses the *Treasuries* have inherited from the magazine are private homes, practically none of whose interior views had ever been published before, and probably none at all in color as they are today. In the present book alone, more than half of the outstanding early homes illustrated are houses whose interiors are placed on public view only through the pictures published here, except on the rarest occasions. These private homes are among the most distinguished and beautifully maintained early houses in the country. They have been carefully picked for the perfection of their furnishings; and the opportunity these pictures present the reader is one made possible only through the courtesy and patience of the many owners, all acknowledged by name in another part of the book, who were kind enough to share their possessions freely for this purpose.

All the other houses that appear in this book are houses that are regularly open to the public and maintained for that purpose. There are approximately 1,000 such early houses in the country, from modest historical shrines, often beautifully kept in far out-of-the-way places, to houses of such great elegance and fame as Mount Vernon itself. And it is from the attendance figures at these open houses that we know the number of people who visit them every year. A careful sampling of these houses, large and small, indicates that altogether they are visited annually by well over twelve million people. This would make them appear to be one of the most popular attractions that the great American public goes out of its way to see. The 1955 figures on Mount Vernon alone were 1,096,302. No one who has visited Williamsburg at the height of the season would ever need figures to describe the crowds of fascinated sightseers at that stunning exhibition town. And far up in Vermont, still comparatively unknown except among connoisseurs, the little museum village of Shelburne attracted 30,000 paid admissions from June through October in the very first year of its existence. To Sturbridge Village, in Massachusetts, more than 120,000 came in 1955; four times as many as five years before. Likewise, every early open house from which figures could be obtained made it clear that the number of visitors was mounting rapidly year after year.

There is still another manifestation of the pleasure and interest taken by the public in the fine early homes of this country, and that is the organized annual pilgrimage or tour, which is now to be met up with from Natchez, Mississippi, to Kittery, Maine. The Natchez event, and the ones that combine the beauties of spring and early architecture from there through New Orleans, Mobile and Charleston to the great state-wide tours in Virginia and Maryland, are not only the largest, but having been at it the best able to furnish figures on their yearly attendances, which for 1954 totaled well over 200,000 traveling devotees.

At this point it is opportune to mention that one book which has been forever missing from that long shelf beside us, but which will not be missing much longer after the *Treasury* appears, is a book which tells how to find all the houses, and what they are like. Not only the many hundreds of houses open to the public, but all the fine early houses that, as private homes, can be seen on the various annual house tours and pilgrimages. Such a book, with descriptive listings of the houses, state by state, has long been in preparation by the authors of this *Treasury*. For while attendance is tremendous at the open houses and at the annual house tours, it is as nothing compared with what it might become when a guidebook is at hand to give complete directions.

Already the figures are fairly staggering. For when you add to the millions of *Journal* readers who follow the Regional Series in the magazine the even more millions of visitors every year to the houses themselves, you have a sizable segment of our population. Does it come as a surprise to the reader of this book that out of these houses so many people seem to be getting an esthetic kick, an historical thrill? And getting at the same time a satisfied curiosity, not only as to the way early Americans lived but as to the way living Americans live now in early American houses?

We can remember a time when many of the houses now looking so beautiful in this book were in danger of destruction, just from neglect, lack of interest. And don't think the danger is past, by any means. And for anyone eager to help avert it, there are organizations doing a wonderful job of preservation.

All will agree with what the Goulds said at the outset of the Regional Series, that "Here in this country, instead of palaces, temples, tombs or cathedrals, the real historical monuments are the fine old homes that tell the history of our American people."

For these homes are a living reminder of our heritage. The people who built and lived in the houses you see here are the people who made this country what it is—strong, free and unafraid. Not only are the houses an inheritance of beautiful and sturdy architecture, but they give us a vivid picture of a society in which independence of mind and honesty of workmanship were regarded as the highest qualities, and men expressed these qualities in the way they built and lived.

# CONTENTS

# INTRODUCTION

IF when you pass into the pictorial part of this book you have taken your itinerary from the table of contents, you will find yourself turning from house to house on a north to south journey through regions unbelievably rich in early American houses. And needless to tell you, the territory through which you travel mostly will be that of the Thirteen Original Colonies.

You will be starting in the state of Maine—perhaps farther off to the eastward in Maine than you might have expected; and from there you will work your way right on down to Georgia, ending up with a side excursion over into Tennessee. On this trip through the *Treasury* you will have stopped to look at fifty-seven houses in thirteen states and the District of Columbia; taken in a total of a hundred and forty-odd interiors.

And what a nice orderly and simple progression it makes as we contemplate these pages. The way it worked out in actuality, however, was this: that each house, each place, was a project all its own. Sometimes it was north, sometimes south. Each house was two trips; one to reconnoiter, one to take pictures. First to find it, then to photograph it, and still to sit down and get it ready for the reader. No wonder it takes five years to fill a *Treasury*!

When we finally reached the point of putting them all together in a book, there was a choice, whether to set forth the houses in terms of time or in terms of locality. We thought of the way people who like to look at houses go from place to place; and then of how history proceeds from date to date. The former seemed a little more fun. And as we wanted this to be as much as possible a pleasure book, we decided to let the order of the houses here be based not so much on *when* they were built, as *where*. The period of a house was something you could take in your stride. It would be time enough as we came to each house in its rightful place along the way, to put each house in its proper place in history.

Having now led you to expect that each house here will be shown as being just where it was built, let us pause to explain that this will not always turn out to be the case. Some of the houses, you will discover, have come a long way from home. There is naturally nothing new about taking a house to pieces in one place and putting the pieces together again somewhere else. Nothing new, even, about lifting a house up bodily and setting it down at a distance. This type of transference has been going on ever since the temples of the ancients. But it has now become such common practice in this country that it takes on the character of collecting; and by means of it various restoration villages on the order of Shelburne and Sturbridge are being augmented each in its own attractive, instructive and often fascinating fashion, as will be seen at some future time in a further volume of the *Treasury*.

As to the houses in this book which have been less than stationary, the movings have been varied. The shortest haul was that given to Dumbarton, at Georgetown, which was disassembled brick by brick and re-erected less than a hundred yards away, to let a street go through. The longest was when The Lindens was dismantled at Danvers, Massachusetts, transported on a fleet of trucks to Washington, D.C., and put together again there on Kalorama Road. Whereas in a way the most spectacular undertaking of any was the voyage made by Spite House, all in one piece, on two great barges, from Phippsburg up the Kennebec, around by open sea to Rockport, Maine, where it stands now, enchantingly resettled on shore.

So you will come upon houses here which will not have been as immobile as they look. And although there are people who would appear to deplore the procedure, the houses we know have always been made better off by it. What Danvers lost when The Lindens left, it was destined to lose by gradual disappearance anyway, for the house was on the point of being disposed of, panel by panel, mantel by mantel, door by door. And the gain to the Washington street where The Lindens now stands has been great; for in a neighborhood of comparatively recent mansions that in appearance approach the palatial, this truly manorial house from Massachusetts, without seeming to try, turns out to be the stateliest of all. No one can miss in The Lindens' new setting the lesson it provides in good early architectural manners.

If you were to guess that the houses in this book had been chosen for their age and their charm together, you would be close to correct. It was also important for our purpose that they should be beautifully dressed. That makes quite a rare combination of qualities to encounter. Charm is partly a thing of chance; a quality that no amount of determined effort alone is able to achieve. Given certain ingredients, certain touches, and there it is. You walk into the living room of Troth's Fortune, in Talbot County, Maryland (a county of incredible charm), and you see it in its subtlest form; the effect being of something absolutely effortless, which is exactly what it wasn't.

Then there is the thing of period perfection, which is another matter entirely. It can be lovely and exciting, and it can be on the other hand altogether lacking in charm. The houses here that are examples of period perfection were chosen—do we have to say?—because we thought they were charming as well. Look at the House of History for this, or look at The Lindens again.

And some were chosen because they dramatically demonstrated how bold the early builders and furnishers were with their interior colors; the theory having been long since exploded that all "colonial" pigments were pale. Of this there could hardly be a better example than the Brush-Everard in Williamsburg, where everything has the bright ring of authenticity and the showmanship casts a sheen of pure delight.

And the attributes of stunning style and pleasing proportions were reasons for making still other choices, all to be combined of course with age and glamour as disclosed in the Charleston interiors, and in those of Kenmore at Fredericksburg, and of the Lady Pepperrell at Kittery.

We seem to be acting as host and hostess at a party, introducing our guests. And it *is* like a party, getting all these houses together here for the first time in a book. But let there be no mistake about any two of them being alike. There are what we find ourselves calling personality houses, which would be houses that reflect almost hypnotically the presence and character of many generations of a family, like the Rundlet-May in Portsmouth. And when we say that these are the least alike of any, we have to say in truth that every house we know is a personality house—each house a personality.

Its date has a lot to do with its design appearance. Its looks in that respect reflect the fashion of its time. Yet honestly we feel that the houses gathered here in the *Treasury* are less to be identified by date than by the kind of people who were their owners and builders, by the places where they were built, and how and of what they were made. In the picturing of an early house, an often more important point to make than how old it looks is how young. Keeping the beauty of a house alive is to keep alive the house itself. For the fact, in that sense, that all the houses here are alive, credit the people who own and occupy them now.

And credit countless others like them for the fact that in five years from now there will still be far too many equally fine early American homes for still another *Treasury* to contain.

# THE
# SECOND TREASURY
## OF
## *Early American Homes*

# The Elegance of Early Maine

THE RUGGLES HOUSE IN COLUMBIA FALLS; SPITE HOUSE NEAR ROCKPORT;

THE TATE HOUSE IN STROUDWATER OUTSIDE PORTLAND;

THE LADY PEPPERRELL MANSION AT KITTERY

IN the Ruggles house the solo part was played by a woodcarving carpenter whose name should not have been forgotten. Like the virtuoso performing in a concerto, he created his own cadenzas. The one for the hallway, which takes your breath away as you enter the house, is the *tour de force* of a flying divided staircase that faces you here. And the one for the drawing room is the mantelpiece of pure inspiration you are coming to.

It is stated somewhere without too much conviction that the villagers of Columbia Falls, watching him at work, came to consider that the carver's knife he held was guided by the hand of an angel. They also thought he had come there from England, in which case the angel might have been embodied in the brothers Adam; for as you will see, it is their fashion that he followed, though the style is entirely his own. In any event, with the staircase he demonstrated his understanding of design, to a most unusual degree, and with the mantelpiece a rare freshness of feeling for decoration.

The man on whose house he lavished all this skill and taste was Thomas Ruggles, who had come in 1795 from Rochester, Massachusetts, to what was then known as the District of Maine. Securing a large timber grant, he proceeded to make his fortune. When this was accomplished, he decided in 1816 to build a house for himself in Columbia Falls which would be somewhat out of the ordinary. It was not an unusual decision for a man to make when he finds himself with the right amount of money; and it is certainly one that has accounted first and last for a lot of fascinating architecture, as indicated here.

Although at Columbia Falls you are getting quite close to Canada, Ruggles sent the whole way back to Duxbury, in his home state, for a carpenter-architect named Aaron Sherman who, as it happened, had just

done a house there for Daniel Webster. It is tantalizing not to know why Ruggles decided to do this. Anyway, it will give us a chance to reconstruct in our minds at least his architect's journey to Maine.

On his way to Columbia Falls, Sherman would almost certainly have had to come through Kittery, and there have stopped to look at the Lady Pepperrell mansion, which you yourself will shortly see here. And fifty miles farther along, just before passing through Portland, you can be sure he paused professionally at the Tate house; and if he had a nose for what was new and good in architecture, he would have seen Spite House, too, which had just been built at Phippsburg.

He still had a long way to go; and as he got farther and farther from Massachusetts Bay, we wonder what he thought when the houses kept on being so fine, and the fine ones so plentiful. We wonder what he thought, for instance, when he went through Wiscasset. Not that he could have seen anything finer than the Tate and the Pepperrell and Spite House all the wonderful way from Kittery to Columbia Falls. Or for that matter anything finer than the house he was about to build there for Mr. Ruggles. Or could anyone today, as far as that's concerned.

THE RUGGLES HOUSE. On his way, Mr. Ruggles' architect-carpenter must have noted well the four-square form and low-hipped roof which marked the more substantial everyday dwellings he passed. For in the Ruggles house he has caught, of course, those familiar regional features, here distinguished by many unusual delicacies of decoration and design, due no doubt in part to his collaboration with the talented wood-carving carpenter whose name no one remembers.

*The Staircase in the Ruggles House*

*The Ruggles House, in Columbia Falls: 1816*

Over the windows on the outside of this faraway house the carved swags center in a heart. If ever a house was built with a woman in mind it is this one, and one imagines a woman of elegant taste at that. Whatever the significance of the hearts, the owner, who moved into his new house in 1818, was to enjoy his exquisite home for a tragically brief time. He died there in 1820.

The house remained in the Ruggles family until 1922. Even when they could no longer afford to hold it, they refused to sell it until the Ruggles House Society, formed to preserve it, put into the deed that no part of the house should ever be removed from Columbia Falls. The house has the good fortune to have as custodian Mary Ruggles Chandler, a direct descendant of the original owner.

The Society has furnished the house with appropriate pieces that point up the lightness and delicacy of the rooms. But it is the dazzling decoration of the superb chimney piece which, right after the staircase, catches the eye of the visitor who has been driving for hours through blueberry moors past sober down-East farmsteads. Its cabinetry of cherrywood on white is said to have taken two years to carve, with all its lacelike delicacies. It hardly

*Spite House, in Rockport: 1806*

*The Ruggles Drawing Room*

matters how long it took. The man must have known he was working on his masterpiece.

SPITE HOUSE. In 1806, in the village of Phippsburg Center, seven miles down the Kennebec from Bath, a well-to-do young sea trader named Captain Thomas McCobb, commanding the best of builders' books and ship-carpentry talent, put up this house to get back at his widowed stepmother for something she did or didn't do—it doesn't matter which any more. Up to then, her own occupancy of the McCobb family mansion close by carried with it considerable éclat, for it had been the finest house in all that part of Maine. But the magnitude and eye appeal of Thomas' new home were such as to set the older house completely in the shade and dim its prestige. That this had been Thomas' intention all along, in the minds of his neighbors, accounts for the name his house took on and still retains.

In 1925, Spite House caught the eye of a connoisseur able to have it loaded on an enormous barge and towed eighty miles up the coast to a wooded knoll on Deadman's Point at Rockport. And a good thing it is for the stepmother's ghost that it was taken so far away from Phippsburg. For what had been mere handsomeness before is magnificence now.

The dining room, page 18, whose French doors open into one of the many beautiful gardens which surround the house, is papered in *Dufour* French wallpaper depicting Pizarro's conquest of Peru, in colors as brilliant as though they had been blocked yesterday. The carpet and the cornice are *tours de force* of reproduction—the former from an 1820 carpet found in New England, probably a Brussels, the latter from the famous Cavanaugh-Cabot house at nearby Newcastle.

In the drawing room, page 19, the owners have carried their vaseline glass candlesticks around the corner of the

17

*The Spite House Dining Room*

mantelpiece to draw your attention to the fact that the mantel returns on the chimney wall, a rare architectural detail found in some of the finer homes of this section of New England, as you can observe for yourself in this book. Color treatment of woodwork in this room is as close as possible to the original paint, the outlining of moldings helps to bring out its crisp yet sturdy character. To the right of the desk is a painting of Captain Thomas McCobb, done in 1802, four years before the house was built. The fact that Captain McCobb had lived through a scalping by pirates who boarded his ship, and that he carried a silver plate in his skull, could hardly be guessed

from the serenity of his expression. Looking beyond him into the hall, the drape wallpaper can be seen, a small piece of the original having been found on the wall and exactly copied for the owners.

In the large, airy bedroom, over the drawing room, whose furnishings are "punkin pine," color again is the essence of livable charm. The hooked rugs and dark green Sandwich glass—of both of which the house has a museum collection—pick up the fresher greens in wallpaper and silk drapery. Again you see in this room the unusual mantel which is characteristic of this section of the coast.

*A Spite House Bedroom*

*The Spite House Drawing Room*

*The Tate House, near Portland: 1775*

*The Lady Pepperrell Mansion, in Kittery: 1760*

TATE HOUSE. When George Tate came here in 1775 as Mast Agent to King George the Fourth and Purveyor to His Majesty's Forests, this is the house he built for himself and his family in Stroudwater, then a village of thirteen other houses, and now a part of Portland. As is pointed out by the Maine Society of Colonial Dames, who have beautifully and understandingly restored it, the site chosen for the house by Tate was most strategic, since it overlooked in front the Mast Landing on the Fore River, where logs were loaded on the King's vessels, and in the rear the Stroudwater River, which flows into the Fore River from the northwestern forests.

The rather remarkable roof, because of its gambreled gables and recessed continuous dormer, provided rooms in the attic which were both light and commodious for the house slaves. Many of the clapboards on the front are the original ones with feathered edges, and the weathered walls are weathering still, as they have been doing now for nearly two hundred years.

Outside, the house has the air of a rather modest dwelling, but within it has certain elegant features that befitted His Majesty's representative. One of these is the beautiful paneling throughout. In the dining room, page 22, the black line you see above and along the top of the bolection molding cornice was discovered as part of the original paint job, the colors of which have been carefully uncovered and faithfully followed throughout the house. To the person looking into the hallway at the delightful staircase, the bold diamond pattern on the floor is almost startling and might be mistaken for a modern note. But it is exactly as it was when the Tates went in and out the heavy front door.

THE LADY PEPPERRELL MANSION. There is every reason in the world for calling it that, for to have an imposing residence built for herself was the first thing the widow Pepperrell decided to do after the death of Sir William. It was apparently Lady Pepperrell's well-carried-out wish that the façade should be so delightfully grande dame, for it is said that she sent to England for her carpenters. It could be that the house furnishes a clue to her character, for even after the Revolution had rendered her title null and void, she demanded unavailingly that she be addressed with the deference she still fancied to be her due. A stickler for architectural correctness might query certain features of the mansion, but the nobility of the house itself has never been disputed.

Lady Pepperrell's elegant parlor, it is certain, must have looked then much as it does today, for we are told that the tea table was always set, and we know that the portrait above the mantel is lovely Jane Pepperrell, youngest sister of Sir William, who probably occupied the same central panel she does now. The small portrait between the windows is a choice Peale, the subject unknown.

The proportions of this room, with its fine overmantel and dentil cornice, are particularly pleasing. The long, deep-set windows with paneled shutters form inviting seats, framed, as they are, with heavy golden damask which sets the rich tone for the room—a tone soft, warm and feminine, befitting a lady of quality. The tinkling crystal candelabra on the Duncan Phyfe table, the inlaid tea chest and beautiful Chippendale mirror above it, ornaments, china and rugs from the Orient, complete the picture of affluence and pride which the whole house expresses with such effectiveness.

*The Lady Pepperrell Parlor*

*The Lady Pepperrell Dining Room*
*In the stately dining room with its painted black-and-white floor, the woodwork is a two-tone treatment which shows off the unusual paneling; the moldings as well as the slight slant of the floor indicate the work of ship carpenters. Lowestoft china, including chocolate cups, graces a handsome mahogany Duncan Phyfe dining table, over all of which the little "Countess of Oxford" by Hoppner looks sweetly down from her place in the panel above the fireplace. The drop-leaf dining table is a good American Chippendale made in 1760 and has fluted legs. The chairs are the same vintage.*

21

*A Tate House Bedroom*

*The west bedroom has a cupboard in the paneling for wigs. The bedspread of copperplate is something that connoisseurs will recognize at once as rare. The hooked rug, the rush-seated rocker and the small Windsor complete the kind of thoughtful treatment which marks the houses of the Colonial Dames all over the country.*

*The Tate House Dining Room*

*The Rundlet-May House, in Portsmouth: 1807*

# Portsmouth Mansion

## THE RUNDLET-MAY HOUSE

PORTSMOUTH MANSION, or the "Manshon House," as James Rundlet called it in his meticulously kept account books which contain every item connected with the building of his house, along with other matters of interest concerning the life of a merchant in the Portsmouth of that day.

To go directly to the Rundlet record for details, we are told that in the first purchase in August 1806 were 7,146 feet of boards and planks and a mast for $75 (the mast for special planking, as for "window stools"). At the same time were purchased 4,000 feet of boards and planks for $52 and 6,000 feet "clear" for $120.

In April 1807 he paid William Tucker $7.20 for "blowing rock," and now at last, he was ready to start digging. It took eight men to excavate for the cellar and, at the rate of a dollar a day, they received in all $73.91. Now again Mr. Rundlet had to buy lumber. And the chimney was begun. By October things were really moving along, the house had been framed and the joiners were at work. Their board alone, at $3 a week, came to $212.50 that fall. They must have come from a distance, for otherwise they would hardly have needed to be "boarded." Nor did they live by board alone; for what about the entry for "45 gal-

lons of rum for workmen this past summer—$45"? But rum and brandy are frequent items in the accounts, it having been the custom for an employer to supply them, and in a tidy quantity too.

Mr. Ralph May, the present owner and great-grandson of Mr. Rundlet, says that he has wondered at the ability of his ancestor to pay out these large sums in cash. But he comes to the conclusion that many of the carpenters were customers of Rundlet's, and therefore it was likely that relatively small amounts of cash were actually exchanged. Mr. Rundlet, as one of the leading merchants of the town, had a tempting stock of linens, woolens, carpets and coffee; as well as extra long silk gloves, not to mention rum from St. Croix and "Fashionable Beaver Bonnetts." Let us hope the workmen took home long silk gloves and Beaver Bonnetts to their waiting wives, instead of squandering their credit on additional libations.

By May 1809, after two years in the building, the house was ready and James and Jane moved in. And in spirit it can be said that they have never moved out. For in every sense of the word, here is a house that has really "remained in the family."

*The Rundlet-May Drawing Room*

Some of the furniture in these rooms was handed down from the first Rundlets, some acquired by later generations of the family; all, of course, antiques today. The Number 9 Rumfort Roaster is still in the kitchen. Much of the original hardware and glass is still in place, as is the lovely rose wallpaper with its border of daisies in the living room. The large portrait of a young lady in this room represents Louisa Catherine Rundlet May, daughter of James and Jane Rundlet and one of their thirteen children who grew up here. Note the knight's lance curtain-poles which were made for the first window hangings. Across the hall from this much-lived-in room, is the sitting room shown opposite, whose marble fireplace is imposed under

the original wooden mantel, for later more efficient heating, it may be assumed. On the left-hand side of it sits a double silhouette of the first owners. The pair of Hepplewhite love seats are unique and priceless. The over-all effect of these rooms is indescribably reminiscent of all the people who have loved living here.

Upstairs, the bedroom shown opposite contains the master's mahogany four-poster, with its lovely old toile covering repeated in chair and drapery; the bed having been bought in 1802 for $21, before the house was built. Its cream and gilt painted cornice, of which you can see only a corner, was part of the original fitting, and matches the delicately ornamented cornices over the windows.

24

*A Rundlet-May Bedroom*

*The Rundlet-May Parlor*

# A Massachusetts Miscellany

A SHAKER HOUSE AT RICHMOND; THE OLD HEATH HOUSE IN BROOKLINE;

GORE PLACE AT WALTHAM; TWO HOUSES ON NANTUCKET;

COGSWELL'S GRANT NEAR ESSEX;

THE JEREMIAH LEE MANSION IN MARBLEHEAD

SHAKER HOUSE. Near this house at Richmond is one of the few surviving Shaker communities in the country, remnants of a religious sect whose "Believers" lived and worked with such a passion for pure simplicity that the furniture and household wares they made, when the movement was flourishing a hundred years ago, are now cherished by connoisseurs as prime examples of meticulous American craftsmanship, unexcelled for utilitarian beauty and unadorned perfection of design. Within the house itself, as will be seen on succeeding pages, a most remarkable assembly of these Shaker furnishings fills the chaste interior, the plainness of whose plastered walls and unaffected woodwork provides just the unpretentious setting these pieces require. All of which comes about because Dr. and Mrs. Edward D. Andrews, whose home it is, are our foremost authorities on Shaker culture, students of its art and literature and discriminating collectors.

THE OLD HEATH HOUSE. In contrast is the patrician manner of this house in Brookline. Among all the many fine early homes of America which were built by fond parents as wedding presents for their young marrieds, this is one of the happiest examples we know; it having been handed down from one generation to another, beginning with that of young Ebenezer Heath who carried his bride across its brand-new threshold in 1791. It was one of the great beauties of the whole Boston neighborhood at the time, and still is. It started right off being a house that everyone enjoyed tremendously. Young Mr. Heath would come trooping in after town meeting with his fellow selectmen. He played the clarinet, the flute, cornet and drum. He also sang for dancing when the fiddlers failed to appear. The house was always full. It was full of attractive young ladies one afternoon in 1825 when the elderly Lafayette stopped by and kissed

*Shaker House, near Richmond:*
*Early Nineteenth Century*

*The houses outside were as simple and plain as the rooms within, though not having received the same close and intimate attention as the furniture, fabrics and utensils, they perhaps never acquired the extraordinary style, very modern in feeling, of the things in daily use indoors.*

*The Old Heath House, in Brookline: 1791*

*Gore Place, at Waltham: 1804*

them all. A little later it was a house to which Emerson would come for its Friday evenings of music; one of the young Heaths playing the French horn in the ensemble, and Abigail Heath playing one of the first pianos in Brookline. . . . The old Heath house is not the first Heath house that has stood in this same locality. It is the third. Perhaps it should really be called the *young* Heath house.

GORE PLACE. Continuing the contrasts that the early homes of Massachusetts provide in apparently endless numbers, we come to the queenly elegance of Gore Place, still part of the Boston neighborhood. As recently as the thirties, it was described as being run as a tearoom and restaurant. That it has now been rescued possibly from fates even worse, if not final, and restored to the grandeur of its great days, is due to the efforts of the Gore Place Society, and of Mrs. F. Gordon Patterson, its director.

Five years after it was built, in 1809, on the morning after Christopher Gore was elected Governor of Massachusetts, seventy-five of his friends arrived on horseback here at his Waltham country seat to wish him well. They couldn't have come to a house better able to handle so many celebrants, as certain of its interiors farther along will make doubly clear. This happens to be Gore Place number two. For it was during the Gores' long stay in London, where he became American chargé d'affaires, that their first house here burned down, and there are good reasons for believing that Gore got the famous Sir John Soane to design this new one. At any rate, the new house went up while the Gores were still in London—a wonderful job, whoever did it. What it would cost to build today is a frightening thought; but what it cost in 1804 was $23,000. Why, you couldn't begin to build the little Shaker house for that!

SHAKER HOUSE. In its rooms (pages 28 and 29) the Andrews have re-created the order and peace that were a requisite of all Shaker communities. Everything must be plain and utilitarian and everything must be well-made, but color was by no means excluded. In the stoutly beamed living room the Andrews have painted the floors Shaker red and the doors and window frames green-blue, which makes an authentic background for the wash bench, the slat-back chairs, the candelabra hanging from the ceiling, the brown pottery and the diminutive wood-burning stove—all of course made by the Shakers. The hand-woven strip carpeting is part of the perfection.

As is proper, the kitchen overlooks a vegetable and herb garden. As you will see, herbs were most important. In the corner is a marble sink on a wooden frame. The "Believers" built cupboards and drawers into the walls of both their dwellings and shops. The wooden kitchen utensils, dishes, bowls, ladles, as well as the baskets and herb containers hanging from the ceiling, are all of Shaker origin, made stoutly for wear, and made with care and precision, because honest craftsmanship was part of their creed.

Running the length of the house in back is a long room or gallery (once a weave room), which now serves as dining and breakfast room. Paneled with wide painted pine boards, the gallery is furnished with a ten-foot trestle table, a bench with a back which is also a chest, and straight chairs. At the farther end can be seen a drop-leaf table and an unusual cupboard, a large pine piece of excellent proportions, which once served in a Shaker dispensary or "nurse shop" for the herbs, which, for the most part, comprised their medications.

Here you also get what would have been a rare glimpse into a second-floor "retiring" room as it was

*The Shaker House Sitting Room*

called, where there is a typical cot on wooden rollers, covered by a bedspread with an unexpectedly bold pattern. In front of the rocking chair is a step-stool, and there is also a sister's sewing stand, and a mirror-on-rack for those so worldly as to wish to see themselves. All in all it is a house whose purity of feeling reflects the life and labors of the small sect of "Believers" who inspired it.

T HE OLD HEATH HOUSE. It is a house full of things that have been there from the beginning. The little child's chair in the keeping room (page 30), which you will probably notice first of all, is a hundred and fifty years older than the house itself, and has been handed down in this family for over three hundred years.

The other two rooms downstairs are more elegant. The paneled library shown on page 31 contains, beside its Queen Anne and Chippendale furniture, some of the owners' collection of ancient East Indian art. The bronze head over the bookcase has been called by experts one of

*A Shaker House Bedroom*

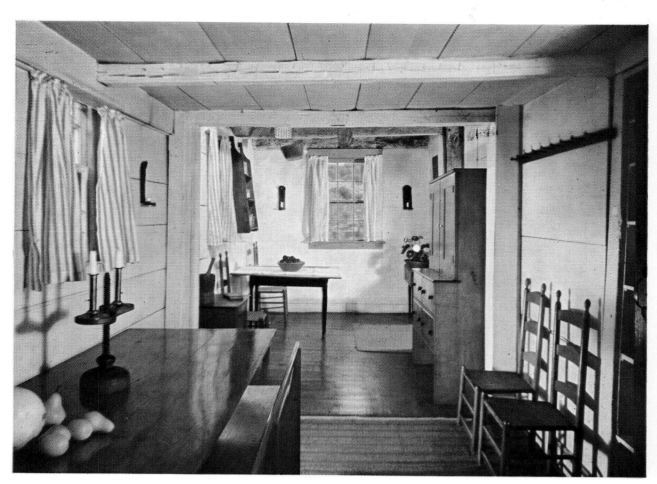

*The Shaker House Dining Room*

*The Shaker House Kitchen*

*The Old Heath House Keeping Room*

the greatest works of its period. You can see quite well the terra-cotta head on the table in the foreground, and smaller figurines are scattered here and there throughout the house. The English bookcase has always stood where it stands; the game of draughts set out on the gaming table is the one with which the selectmen of Brookline played when the house was new and Brookline a village.

The bedroom over the library (page 31) has much the same type of fireplace paneling, on the bed the linsey-woolsey quilted spread that beautifully belongs there. Bed and window draping is fine muslin finished in hand-netted fringe. The dish-top table in the window

is Queen Anne, as is also the tall-backed chair made by Joseph Short of Newburyport when the house was young. There is a feeling of a fine tradition continuing through the centuries of this house—as vigorous and alive today as ever.

GORE PLACE. To give you an idea of the size of this mansion, there are five entertainment rooms on the first floor, similar in size to the state dining hall pictured on page 32; and that takes care of only one wing. Up a stunning spiral staircase from the great entrance hall there are guest rooms galore, for children as well as

*An Old Heath House Bedroom*

*The Old Heath House Library*

*The Gore Place Banquet Hall*

for grownups. The Gores being childless, they always liked having the house full of nieces and nephews. Endless people coming in from Boston stayed to dine and spend the night. The state dining room was used for exactly what its name implies, there being a smaller one for the family and their friends—though small is hardly what even that one would be called. The dentiled cornice and fine Adam mantel add to its great elliptical elegance. The pedestal mahogany banquet table, whose length accommodated many world-famous citizens of the time, and the spoon-back Queen Anne chairs were of American make, as were the drop-leaf side tables to match.

Over them hang portraits of the Governor's parents. The mantel, further graced by an Empire gilt mirror, reflects a chandelier once belonging to Daniel Webster, who read law in Mr. Gore's office. The uncovered marble floor and the flags of the nation and state, always used on important occasions, complete a room whose dignity bespeaks the importance of its owner.

The drawing room, which occupies the whole end of the right-hand wing, is a room which any family might have enjoyed, for its high fan windows make it a brightly sunlit salon. The furnishings are gay too. The unusual mirror over another Adam mantel, with its lovely landscape

32

*A Gore Place Bedroom*

above, is an English piece, as are others of the pictures, the fire screen, and some of the furniture.

You pass through many rooms and corridors on your way to the Gores' own bedroom, which occupies the right-hand corner of the high part of the house. It is a delightful room off which the Governor had his private study. Here the mahogany bed is Adam and unusually fine, the folded coverlet quilted of silk. The large pattern in the hand-blocked wallpaper suits the big scale of the room and seems to reflect the greens in the lovely park outside the windows. The chaise longue at the foot of the bed is English but the rest of the furniture is American; and many of the accessories, together with the trunk and sewing table, belonged to the Gores.

*The Gore Place Drawing Room*

*West Brick, Middle Brick and East Brick, on Nantucket: 1838*
*In 1838, a wealthy whaling-fleet owner named Joseph Starbuck built three identical brick houses side by side on Main Street, one for each of his sons. By far the most impressive in Nantucket, they have always been known as West Brick, Middle Brick and East Brick—reading from left to right.*

*The Dell House, on Nantucket: c. 1800*
*There is no one such thing as a typical Nantucket house, yet all the old houses there are in some harmonious way inescapably typical of Nantucket; and none more than this picturesquely austere captain's house on a hilltop overlooking the ocean.*

34

TWO HOUSES ON NANTUCKET. Twenty miles out from the coast of Cape Cod, the island of Nantucket rises unbelievably beautiful from the sea. The town, with its clustered harmony of handsome old houses, drifts off into long stretches of creamy cliffs and gray-green moors. The old section still contains 400 houses antedating the great fire of 1846 which largely burned out the dwellings of the central district, most of which were immediately replaced by new ones which even today are considered somewhat newish by the Islanders.

Of these, which are what the visitor sees as he strolls through the winding streets and lanes of the town where they still stand as tightly ranked and close to the pavement as they stood from the beginning, many were rebuilt in exactly the same style as those destroyed by the holocaust. You see the same steep roof slopes and four-bay scheme of the earliest settlers which were described by de Crèvecoeur in 1782 as "entirely devoid of exterior or interior ornament, lathe plastered within, handsomely painted and boarded without."

At the period of the great fire, the town was at the peak of its whaling prosperity, and when it was rebuilt a few of the wealthy merchants and sea captains preferred the opulent Greek Revival fashion, both for homes and public buildings, a style by that time much in vogue on the mainland. Then, too, the brick houses, shown here, built a little before the fire, in 1835–37, in the Federal fashion of earlier Salem mansions, also reflected a departure from Quaker simplicity. However, they, as well as the Greek Revival buildings, partake of the general air of conservatism and restraint with the result that all three periods look well together. Observers from Crèvecoeur to the last summer visitor to step off shore in 1954 characterize the feeling of Nantucket as "harmonious."

*East Brick Library*

*An East Brick Bedroom*

Talbot Hamlin describes Nantucket as "one of the most harmonious and attractive of American seaport towns. The effect of the town as one strolls through it," he says, "is exactly that intended by its builders of a century ago . . . there is a definite sense of composition, of harmony in design, a careful choice of materials . . . the living expression of community life as the people of the Greek Revival desired it to be."

But it might have been the spirit of the Islanders themselves rather than the Greek Revival spirit which was responsible for this harmonious effect. More than one hundred and fifty years before that, Crèvecoeur was observing "a scene of uninterrupted harmony," and never tired of singing the praises of "this happy settlement" where good will and industry predominated. To be sure, when he visited these shores it was a town of but 500 dwellings on a sandy spot of 23,000 acres. The house frames, he tells us, were brought by boat from the mainland, for even then the male population was so completely absorbed in the hazardous business of whaling that they had no time to bother with the hewing of the little wood that grew here. In fact, by packet from Maine came most of the lumber and shingles and even the firewood. Second-hand building material was saved and re-used in those early days, as much from necessity as thrift. The scarcity of materials naturally influenced the

*The East Brick Double Drawing Room*

building and also made for simplicity and uniformity.

Due to the male preoccupation with the great fish, Crèvecoeur describes the Island society as a sort of matriarchy, where women, left so much alone, had to transact most of the business as well as take all the responsibility for the household. All descended from the first twenty-seven British proprietors, they were a sturdy and capable breed. Crèvecoeur gives us a peek at one of their more unusual habits. "A singular custom prevails here among the women at which I was greatly surprised," Crèvecoeur writes, ". . . they have adopted these many years the Asiatic custom of taking a taste of opium every morning; and so deeply rooted is it that they would be at a loss how to live without this indulgence; they would rather be deprived of any necessary than forego their favorite luxury." He goes on to say that the sheriff, who is the head man, takes three grains a day after breakfast "without which he would be unable to conduct his affairs."

To one pondering this most fascinating of customs in a society marked by Quaker sobriety, it might appear that the harmonious quality of Island life, so strikingly manifest to all observers in its architecture and town planning, may have derived in part from a society whose harsher realities were pleasingly glossed over by some slight preoccupation with the poppy.

EAST BRICK. The bedroom's massive mahogany four-poster on page 36 was made in 1812, when Nantucket was being besieged by the British. The enchanting chaise longue in white satin and rosewood has been in the house since Victorian days.

The two immense drawing rooms above run right through the full depth of East Brick from front to back—matching marble mantelpieces, wallpaper, window draperies. The wingback chair in chintz is an old Nantucket piece; the portrait by the teacher of Sir Joshua Reynolds.

*The Dell House Parlor*

William Starbuck ran the family business from the library when his brothers went to sea. The Chippendale mirror over the mantel on page 35 depicts the battle between the *Chesapeake* and the *Shannon*, with the portraits of the two captains. What you saw beyond the East Brick library is the elegant dining room.

THE DELL HOUSE. In the colorfully papered Dell parlor above which stands to the left of the entrance doorway, the pine paneling has the ship-carpenter quality of so many Nantucket interiors; the handiwork re-

membered from the more studied and academic designs the Island craftsmen had seen in mainland houses.

COGSWELL'S GRANT. This fine old house, filled with rarities, and a rarity itself, is near the coast at Essex, and just over some low green hills from Ipswich, pictured in the first *Treasury*. In fact, it was by that ancient town in 1634 that the land was granted to John Cogswell, giving the house its name. The land has always done well by the house, even when after more than two hundred years of Cogswell ownership, the prop-

*Cogswell's Grant, at Essex: Late Eighteenth Century*

erty was bought in 1839 by a local shipbuilder named Adam Boyd. For Mr. Boyd proceeded to let the place support itself most decoratively by raising acres of peacocks whose meat sold in the Boston market for $1 a pound. It was Mr. Boyd who also planted the now huge and handsome elms that shade the house. The earthy pigment for yellow ocher which produced a weather paint, preferred to white by many a practical-minded early settler for his colonial dwelling, still keeps this rare old farmhouse a mellow pumpkin color.

Everything in the house is choice and still its extraordinary livability leaves no place for the museum look that can happen when so many fine things are present, yet many a museum would like nothing better than to possess the whole house with all it contains.

The painted cedar graining of the woodwork in the best bedroom, which is repeated throughout, wherever it originally existed, shows to best advantage on page 41, where it was carried around the heavy ceiling cornice and the exposed corner posts. In the living room, where the painting cannot be seen in the photograph, the colors are deep green and black. Such woodwork painting was done by early itinerant painters who specialized in it; sometimes it represented the actual graining of certain

*The Jeremiah Lee Mansion, in Marblehead: 1768*

*The Cogswell's Grant Parlor*

woods, sometimes it was intricately combed, mottled, or marbleized. In the living room (see opposite page) the sharp pink in the shell cupboard makes a brilliant contrast to the woodwork and sets forth the earthenware collection; in earlier times this cupboard held the family silver and porringers. The house contains many fine primitive American paintings, the large one here over the butterfly stretcher table is prim Mistress Prudence Waters while opposite is Jane Hutch. Looking past her you can see the dining room, once the kitchen, then through another door under the codfish weather vane to what was formerly the buttery. The handsome country cupboard in the dining room displays a collection of Pennsylvania and Connecticut pottery. Table covers, hooked rug, painted wooden boxes, are all early and completely in keeping.

The somewhat finer woodwork in the best parlor, above, is painted white and sets the room apart with its furnishings as a place for more formal occasions. The Turkish rug, the eighteenth-century harpsichord from London, the Dutch-type chairs with braided seats, the elegant round gaming table with the octagonal marbles board on it—for an early form of solitaire—every touch demonstrates the owners' artistry for nuance.

To return to the bedroom, which is in some ways the chef-d'oeuvre—here the yellow-painted Windsor rocker by the fireplace, the delicate primitive florals in water colors, the faded quilt whose colors blend so perfectly in the ensemble, and by the bed a great blue porcelain foot bath, Chinese export (no doubt brought in by a nearby sea captain)—these things like everything else in this house of many treasures must be savored one by one, for their beauty or interest as separate objects, and then for the effect of the whole. It is also a house you can look at again and again, but only in this book.

*The Cogswell's Grant Living Room*

*A Cogswell's Grant Bedroom*

*The Lee Mansion Kitchen*

THE JEREMIAH LEE MANSION. Colonel Lee had in mind something on the order of a great London town house. He was the wealthiest merchant in Marblehead, and on the side he owned a fleet of sailing vessels that flew his flag from Marblehead to the Orient and back. He wanted his house to be high, so that from a glassed-in cupola on the roof he could catch his sails as they came across the horizon.

These three rooms indicate the opulence of space and finish which prevails throughout the mighty mansion. The upstairs drawing room is certainly one of the most elegant and stately in New England. The ribbon-back straight chairs are Chippendale; the wing chair in antique pale green damask is Queen Anne, as is the tilt-top tea table; the rare tea set is Wheeldon, and the scenic wall-

paper panels of classic ruins were imported from England for the house when it was built.

In the pilastered dining room where on many occasions Revolutionary dignitaries, including Washington and Lafayette, were entertained, the mahogany table and chairs are Hepplewhite; the drop-leaf side table is Sheraton and the goblets are flint glass. Note the elegantly dentiled cornice, the leather fire bucket.

The kitchen here could hardly have been more than a serving-pantry kitchen in Colonel Lee's time, when a separate outside kitchen was customary, and plenty of slaves. The pewter and the paneling are fine, but into the oven you could scarcely squeeze a twenty-pound turkey, let alone the breads, the puddings, and the pots of beans for an establishment of this stature.

*The Lee Mansion Drawing Room*

*The Lee Mansion Dining Room*

43

*The Nightingale-Brown House: 1792*

# Providence in All Its Glory

THE JOSEPH NIGHTINGALE HOUSE;

THE EDWARD CARRINGTON HOUSE;

THE ELIZA WARD HOUSE

SUDDENLY from the bigness and bustle of down-town Providence you come to a kind of residential cliff up which you climb through quiet streetfuls of early brick interrupted now and then by outbursts of splendor, which are houses built after the Revolution rather than before, and represent a twenty-five-year period from roughly 1790 to 1815. They dramatize the prosperity that Providence enjoyed in the days of the early republic, a good part of which came from the city's fabulously rich trade at the time with China, a trade which had its effect upon the furnishings quite considerably in the Carring-ton house, as you will notice.

*The Carrington House: 1810*

NIGHTINGALE-BROWN HOUSE. The house that Joseph Nightingale built in 1792, which is now the home of John Nicholas Brown, stands on its hillside site looking down over present-day Providence. Its tall pedimented Palladian front, topped by a wide balustraded roof, seems to add to the height and breadth of the hill. It is considered to have been designed by a man named Caleb Ormsbee, who had studied to his obvious advantage *A Book of Architecture*, by James Gibbs, the celebrated British architect.

He inherited the book from a leading early amateur architect of Providence, Joseph Brown, whose daughter was the Eliza Brown Ward who built this handsome brick house of hers against the steep Providence hillside some

*The Eliza Ward House: 1813*

*A Nightingale-Brown House Bedroom*

twenty-five years after her father's death, its architect unknown. The high flight of double stairs which led to the original doorway where the bay window now protrudes has long since been removed, and a suitable entrance at street level been substituted.

CARRINGTON HOUSE. Captain Edward Carrington bought his great brownstone mansion in 1812, when it was two years old. Carrington was a Providence merchant of obvious means, a shipowner and shipbuilder to boot. He had also been our consul at Canton, which would help explain that part of his Chinese collection which appears particularly in the pictures on page 48 of his great double drawing rooms. It was he who added a third story to the house, and the tier of porches. The house is being preserved intact, just as it was when the family occupied it, a fact which adds greatly to its interest.

NIGHTINGALE HOUSE. The palatial scale and character of the Nightingale house can be seen from this immense and handsomely furnished bedroom with its exquisite chandelier, yellow damask walls, and its queenly canopied English eighteenth-century four-poster.

The broken-pedimented doorway and the magnificent two-story mantel of the Nightingale drawing room are among the richest examples of late eighteenth-century woodwork in this country, and among the finest features of the house itself. The whole house is lived in; and that it is maintained to perfection goes without saying.

The delicately wrought honeysuckle motif in the frieze section of the great paneled drawing room mantel in the Nightingale-Brown house has been pointed out by Antoinette F. Downing, the architectural historian of Rhode Island, as suggesting the light gracefulness of the Adam style, which soon became so popular in America.

THE CARRINGTON HOUSE. The ample pair of Carrington parlors could hardly be anywhere but in Providence. It took a kind of free-wheeling society to produce it, a tradition of skilled artisans, the trade with China, and fortunes made by free-thinking individuals who were thus able to bring forth their own emphatic architectural style.

*The Nightingale-Brown House Drawing Room*

The Carrington House Double Drawing Room
Although there are double drawing rooms galore not only in this book but in many early American homes not pictured here, probably none is so colorful as this really dramatic pair which Edward Carrington arranged and furnished against the background of his Chinese collections.

*A Carrington House Bedroom*

48

*The Carrington House Double Drawing Room*

*The Ward House Dining Room*

The rare Chinese vases and statues give a unique atmosphere to these rooms, which seem to have been lived in up to yesterday. The lovely peacock wallpaper in the parlor was made in China for the house; the porcelains, the figures, the ivories were all brought back from there by the owner.

The big canopied four-poster (page 48) in one of the Carrington bedrooms carries on the sumptuous feeling of the rooms below. Note the elaborate lacquer chest at the foot; and in the dressing room beyond, on the wall above the Indian clubs, note too that the house is still lighted by gas.

THE ELIZA WARD HOUSE. The spectacular feature of the adjoining parlor and drawing room here is naturally the wallpapers. They were installed soon after

the house was built and just after they were first printed. They are both from the factory of Joseph Dufour in Paris. That in the far room is the "Banks of the Bosphorus," of 1816, composed of landscapes with river and caïques, and consisting of twenty-five strips. That in the near room is commonly known as "Pizarro in Peru," thirty strips, and based on the invasion of 1531, a mad and beautiful savage melee, as romantically depicted here.

The walls of the dining room (see page 49) are covered with the Chinese metallic papers which were used to wrap packages of tea for export. The china in the cupboard is Crown Derby, and the portrait is of the present owner's great-grandmother who rocked her children in the cradle that you may have observed standing in the corner by the shell cupboard.

*The Ward House Living Room and Drawing Room*

*The Webb House, in Wethersfield: 1752*

# The Quality of Connecticut

THE WEBB HOUSE IN WETHERSFIELD; THE NATHAN HALE HOUSE AT SOUTH COVENTRY;

HASTINGS HILL AT SUFFIELD; THE COWLES HOUSES IN FARMINGTON;

THE DENISON HOMESTEAD IN MYSTIC; ANGUILLA AND STONECROP AT STONINGTON;

THE MOWINGS IN MILLINGTON SOCIETY; DUNSTAFFNAGE AT EAST HADDAM;

THE LORD HOUSE IN ESSEX

I
F Washington were to return to Wethersfield today, he would find the Webb house looking very much the same as it did when he visited there in 1781, with only one striking change. For the house now is white, and when he was there before it was a real Connecticut red, like Hastings Hill and Dunstaffnage, a few pages farther along.

The General had come here to confer with the Count de Rochambeau. What was settled here that spring was to lead in the fall to the surrender of Cornwallis at Yorktown, where the negotiations were carried out in the Moore House, which you will find when you come in these pages to Virginia.

When Joseph Webb built the house in 1752, it was his good fortune that he could turn the job over to Connecticut carpenter-craftsmen, who had a special way with wood. For as you climb from cellar to attic, not only do you feel with amazement the original firmness and soundness of the floors and stairways after two hundred years, but you see the original trimness and tightness of the paneling in room after room. The tradition in which the Webb house was built may well be the reason why there

*A Webb House Bedroom*

are more early houses still standing firm and trim in Connecticut than in any other state.

THE WEBB HOUSE. This is a house whose urbanity impresses you the instant you enter the door. You know at once that if you were coming here for tea the conversation would be good. In fact, in the parlor to the left as you enter, the tea table is ready with its Lowestoft all set. The mahogany table is rare Queen Anne dated 1720, the chairs Chippendale and Hepplewhite. Note the hooked rug of unusual size and very fine pattern. The capped and ruched portrait of Sarah Webb Barrell, sister of the first owner, hangs over a Hepplewhite pianoforte which was made in England in 1779.

Add to the satisfying colors in the dining room a paneled chimney wall of great interest with twin cupboards over the mantel, and you have an ideal background for dining. The cupboards are filled with treasures—Newhall,

Royal Crown and Sprig Derby, lots of blue and white Chinese import. Turn to the table and you will see a Wishart silver tea service belonging to the Webb family. The cherry Chippendale chairs were made about 1767 by Connecticut River cabinetmakers. And there is the Eli Terry clock between the windows, also Connecticut of course. It all totals up to a room without pretensions of any kind, but from its paneling and proportions down to its lovely collections of china, a room of distinction.

The room in this house that attracts the greatest attention is the upstairs bedroom shown here. The wallpaper is that which Mr. Webb had put up in preparation for the most important guest he ever entertained—George Washington. The Webbs chose a velvety dark red flock with a rich floral pattern, still handsome against a wall of exceptionally fine paneled woodwork. The large leather chair is said to have been there too, to make everything as comfortable as possible for the Webbs' famous visitor.

*The Webb House Parlor*

*The
Webb House
Dining
Room*

CONNECTICUT sparkles all over with antique towns as carefully tended for the most part as a house full of heirlooms. There are white little hilltop and crossroads communities by the score, still full of prim and true colonial charm. And then there are the handsomely preserved impressive parlor towns like three-hundred-year-old Farmington, whose wide and elmy streets are set with many such fine early homes as the two distinguished neighbors on the opposite page. Using "town" in the original Connecticut sense of a township, you find yourself concerned with whole countryside communities like that of Coventry, in which the Nathan Hale house stands in the village of South Coventry; or like Windsor (one of the richest areas in the state in early houses), where Hastings Hill stands in the village of Suffield; or like Farmington, which in turn contains the considerable town of the same name, already mentioned.

It is quite by chance that Connecticut is rather more heavily represented in this book than any other state, but you can see the coincidence is justified. The range of architectural styles and building methods within the eleven Connecticut houses pictured here represents almost completely the full development of Connecticut houses from the earliest up to those built at the end of the eighteenth century.

Most of the houses here are rich in historical associations. The one known now as the Nathan Hale house was built by the father of Nathan in the momentous year of 1776. Parts of a smaller adjoining house in which the boy was born were built into this one, and, as you will see, the house contains many of the possessions with which he grew up. Unwittingly, what the father was erecting in 1776 was to become in effect a very personal memorial to his soldier son, who was never to live in it as a home. For on a September Sunday morning that year, having been captured behind the British lines in schoolteacher's clothes, he died the death of a patriot spy at the age of twenty, before the house was finished. On its own, the house belongs to the aristocracy of early American country craftsmanship, famous for the nice proportions it produced, and for the everlasting way the everlasting materials were put together. It is a house of fine simplicity and great distinction, kept up today with lived-in fidelity to the man who would have lived in it, and to the times he lived in so briefly.

In the appearance of the red Connecticut farmhouse at Suffield, known as Hastings Hill, there are signs that it started out as a very steep salt-box. The steepness probably was an early carry-over from the steep thatched roofs of England, or even from thatched roofs here; thatching requiring the steeper pitch to shed water more

*The Nathan Hale House, at South Coventry: 1776*

*Hastings Hill, at Suffield: 1737*

*The General Solomon Cowles House, in Farmington: 1782*

*The George Cowles House, in Farmington: 1804*

quickly. When wood shingles came in, a flatter pitch became possible; consequently, by the middle of the eighteenth century roof lines began to change. And some time after that it is conceivable that the roof line of Hastings Hill (opposite page), which was built in 1737, might, too, have changed. Its "punkin pine" sheathing boards were cut from the great stands of yellow pine which grew in the Connecticut Valley when the settlers first came, but which long since have disappeared as timber trees. The color and unpretentiousness of the house are authentic parts of its original simplicity.

HALE HOUSE. The rooms on the next pages have been restored with the patience and devotion which make the house an outstanding evocation of the place and time, and the young man who didn't live to inherit it. In the dining room, with its wall of wide country paneling, the solid old pine table is one at which Washington ate breakfast at nearby Brigham tavern on his way through Coventry. It is set, as it would have been, with pewter and other accessories which actually belonged to Nathan Hale's sister, Joanna. The chubby fireside settee, hard to duplicate anywhere, would have been a cozy fit for two people. Next to it, the frying pan has such a long handle that you wonder how anyone managed to keep it balanced. The strong rush-bottomed chairs are as steady today as they were more than two centuries ago. Things were really made to last for many a lifetime, and the craftsman took pride in the making of even a simple country chair.

In the parlor, the paneled fireplace wall, typical of the solid Connecticut country homes of the period, is finely proportioned. Note that the panels are repeated wafer thin on the inside of the shutters, the reason for whose position is obvious. When the house was built, such shutters were equally necessary for protection against the winter weather, as well as human marauders. The armchair with its back to you is real country Chippendale, and so, in a more comfortable way, is the armchair facing you, upholstered in eighteenth-century damask of a luscious hue. The swags at the windows with the dark fringe are exactly as they would have been, and the materials, as everywhere else in the house, are hard-to-come-by fabrics of the period.

Upstairs in the parlor bed-chamber the interesting feature is the odd heavy piece of cornice above the mantelpiece. This is a lady's room, as the airy four-poster with its graceful tester and its fine chintz and homespun furnishings attests. The blanket chest which has so much style is another Hale heirloom. A Windsor chair and slat-back

*The Hale House Dining Room*

rocker, the old hat box, the candlesticks and five-finger flower vases—every detail adds to the picture of a family and period which has been so skillfully limned in this house.

Hastings Hill. When you come to the living room on page 59 you might be tempted to try the surface of the woodwork to see if it is as lacquer-smooth as it looks. That is the way it is with all the woodwork in the house; it has the polish and glow of a Stradivarius. The room is sheathed in feather-edged pine boards running horizontally on the chimney wall, which is most unusual. By the fireplace is an antediluvian Indian bowl of steatite, found one hundred years ago in North Bradford; the ground of Connecticut having once been rich in Indian artifacts. The slat-back armchair by the fireplace, the seventeenth-

century oak chest with octagonal panels, pottery, candlesticks, lantern on the mantel, are all early Connecticut.

The paneling in the green living room is especially pleasant in its proportions, and beautiful, too, in the way it frames the fine old fireplace. The chair in the left foreground is an early New England bannister-back with elaborate pierced crest, as you can clearly see. The chalk pigeons on the mantel are a bow to the folk art of Pennsylvania, from where these fragile figures come.

In the best bedroom—but they are all best—is a dream of a decorated Connecticut chest. The fireplace chairs are worth your attention, too, the bannister-back with its lovely fan crest and the endearing, prim "necessary" chair are both mid-eighteenth century. It would not be hard to make a copy of the pattern of the linsey-

*A Hale House Bedroom*

*The Hale House Parlor*

*A Hastings Hill Bedroom*

woolsey bedspread in the foreground, but it would take a long time to make it, and of course, where would you find such a color in any new material? An indescribable mustard green which is much like that in some of the exquisite chest painting. The andirons in this room are marked, a real rarity of which the house has certainly its share. The reds and blues are stunning; and now that you have seen it all, we need hardly add that the house is in the hands of a perfectionist.

THE COWLES HOUSES. In 1804, George Cowles and his bride moved into the house whose great hallway and dining room you will see on page 61 as they look

today. The house had been a wedding present from George's father, General Solomon Cowles, who lived down the street in the house whose famous and beautifully paneled living room wall appears on page 60.

The fireplace wall in the general's house is one of the most architecturally contrived in all Connecticut; outstanding for the richness of its detailing, the robustness of its carving. Even the cornerpost, typical of early Connecticut framing, has been costumed in keeping with the rest of the composition, just as the cornerpost in the dining room of Dunstaffnage, on page 70, was made to act as a decorative engaged column. As English-trained craftsmen at the time this house was built, in 1782, were

*The Hastings Hill
Green Living Room*

*The Hastings Hill
Living Room*

*The Solomon Cowles Drawing Room*

generally working with rather more restraint, it is practically certain that this was the creation of American wood-carvers.

In the dining room of the larger and later house—the wedding-gift house—the present owner has done nothing to lessen the splendor of the original appearance. She has let the fine Oriental rug act as a warm foil for the pale walls and soft-blue woodwork. The sideboard is English Hepplewhite, and the painting above it a notable example of its period, called "Coursing in Sussex," by James Ward, R. A. The pastorale above the mantel is by the seventeenth-century Dutchman, van der Meulen. And regard how the great size of the room makes possible the

unusual dining-room luxury of two large and comfortable fireside chairs.

In the practically monumental hallway, a spectacular staircase disappears from view on its way to the high third floor where the formal ballroom used to be. The panels, as you see, are painted in three warm tones in a very successful move to bring the scale of the hall into a pleasantly livable relationship with its use as a living room. The tones are enriched by gilt wall ornaments and by the honey gold in the Chinese rugs and upholstery fabrics. The owner, who has traveled extensively in the Orient, uses many Chinese ornaments in her decor, which suits both her house and her own personality so well.

*The George Cowles Hallway*
*The great staircase hallway and the dining room of the George Cowles house, in the impressiveness of their scale and character, might seem less typical of Connecticut than of Charleston, yet there are several other early houses in the state of similar substance, all attributed, tentatively, to an architect named William Spratt, who may even have done some of the New Bern houses.*

*The George Cowles Dining Room*

*The Denison House, near Mystic*

*A Denison House Bedroom: Nineteenth Century*

**D**ENISON HOUSE. Also known as Pequotesepos Manor, this venerable beauty has been restored in a remarkable fashion, for each of its various rooms has now been made to represent, in its period attire, one of the *eleven* generations of Denisons who have occupied the house. As its historian states, it presents a beautiful and very real panorama of life in Connecticut, from the earliest colonial times to the Gay Nineties. We have chosen two bedrooms of the house to indicate the passage of time in taste from one century to another. Below, the coverlet on the maple four-poster, in which Washington never slept, but in which he would have felt at home, is an Indian hand-printed cotton with the famous tree-of-life design—a true eighteenth-century bedroom. In the Civil

*A Denison House Bedroom: Eighteenth Century*

62

*Anguilla, at Stonington: 1660–1707*

War bedroom on page 62, above, the mahogany sleigh bed and the bureau were made by a member of the Denison family; the Franklin stove to the right is a particularly fine and ornate example.

STONINGTON. On the coast of Connecticut, right next to the Rhode Island line, a community composed of Stonington, North Stonington and part of

Mystic furnishes from its rocky back-country hills these three outstanding examples of the locality's rich array of fine early houses. It is a community in spirit, as well as in fact, made notable by such things as the Stonington Tercentenary, held there in 1949, and the organized efforts that are made to preserve the local landmarks and keep alive the ancient traditions of the neighborhood.

Anguilla, which is one of the oldest houses in the area,

*Stonecrop, at Stonington: 1750*

*The Anguilla Dining Room*

*An Anguilla Bedroom*

not to say one of the oldest in the country, was built by Elisha Cheseborough on part of the first Stonington plantation, settled in 1649 by his father—the first white settler in the Old Pequot Country at a time when this savage easterly coast was claimed by both the Connecticut and Massachusetts colonies. The house was burned and rebuilt in 1707 very much as it now stands, but the stonework of the great chimney, as well as the two paneled fireplaces on the preceding page, is supposed to have withstood the fire, which would make these parts of the present interiors among the oldest in America. It was a big house for its time; the dining room and the bedroom above it (opposite) being twenty feet square and high in proportion, with their size further attested by each room having two summer beams instead of the usual one. The

early furniture is mostly American Queen Anne, mixed in with comfortable contemporary. The drop-leaf oval mahogany dining table and the exquisite marquetry chest-on-stand are eighteenth-century English.

Beyond the beauty and interest of the room as a whole, the kitchen below, in Stonecrop, is notable for the brick "trimmer arch" above the fireplace, a feature found only between Hingham, Massachusetts, and Stonington. The front opening measures seven feet across—not a record, but big enough to boast about.

The owner of the house at the time of the Revolution is said to have taken in seven young volunteers, trained them in tactics, and sent them down to the Fort at New London, making the house, as the present owner likes to put it, the "first officers' training school in the country."

*The Stonecrop Kitchen*

*The Mowings, at Millington Society: Late Seventeenth Century*

# Three Houses Along the Lower Connecticut

BY the time this richly historic stream has separated New Hampshire and Vermont from north to south, cut right across the middle of Massachusetts, and almost met the tides sweeping in from Long Island Sound, it has finally come to the rolling region where the three houses stand which occupy these six pages—all three typical in one way or another of the hundreds that lie back from the river's banks throughout its whole sinuous length from its source to the Sound. No other colonial river—not even the Hudson, the Delaware, the Potomac or the James— was able in the younger years of the country to attract such a quantity of fine houses. Maybe the ones along the Hudson have more variety, just as the ones along the James are more manorial, but for truly native architecture, simple and fine, and for such a vast amount of it, nothing touches the Connecticut.

The Mowings is a late seventeenth-century farmhouse in a once prosperous sawmill community known as Millington Society, far away in a woods filled with pheasant and deer. Owing in part to the roads leading to it, which are still today little more than woodland trails, the house has a feeling of very real remoteness, even from the town of East Haddam on which the community centers. That sense of its remoteness is heightened when you are told that the present owners first heard of their future home during the course of a conversation on colonial houses with some American friends, sitting together on the terrace of the Café du Dôme in Paris. If the house had been more accessible there is no telling what might have happened to it. It was preserved partly by this extreme seclusion, and partly by the poverty of its various occupants after the timbering activities of Millington Society came to an end. Fortunately for the house at least, no one could afford to modernize it; now beautifully demonstrated by the mellow perfection of its interior woodwork, as the pictures point out.

The history of Dunstaffnage—several twisting miles from The Mowings—began when it was built in 1738 by John Warner, a blacksmith from Massachusetts, who came to East Haddam and married a land-rich widow named Mehitable Chapman Richardson. Remodeled in 1790, the house remained in the Warner family until 1880; then there were fifty-odd years of neglect, out of which it has been expertly and handsomely restored by its present owner, who fortunately for the house is both architect and archeologist.

The house has unusually high rough-cut granite foundations, which have been very beneficial of course in preserving the structure. The house is older than it looks as you come up to it from the lawn, due to certain details of the 1790 remodeling, but the steepness of the roof proclaims the fact that it was erected before 1750; and the color it now carries is the same characteristic red of its original earliness.

Fifteen miles down the Connecticut from the East Haddam houses is the charmingly well-kept old river town of Essex, which was settled in 1690 and reached its peak of shipbuilding activity about 1840; by which time Main Street was lined with captains' houses like the Lord house below. Built toward the end of the eighteenth century, this house and most of its contemporaries in the town indicate, by their dentiled cornices and their fine feeling for the architectural fashion of the time, the wealth and worldliness of their seafaring owners.

THE MOWINGS. The sculptor-owner here has spent patient years restoring the mellow patine to the first-growth pine from which his seventeenth-century farmhouse was put together. The great width of the wall boards cut from the wilderness may be seen in the dining room on page 68 and their warm mellow color has its counterpart in the huge table that came from an ancient country cheese factory in Vermont. Not in the picture is the walk-in fireplace that shows this was once kitchen as well as living room. It is still the room in which the owners do most of their living. In the fall of the year, hams, strings of sausages, dried onions and corn festoon the rafters and are gradually consumed.

On the table is part of a collection of wrought-iron candlesticks, some as early as the house, from a time when rushes and fagots, dipped in resin, were used. The country-style rush-bottom chairs are perfect of their kind. The trencher table in the corner comes from an old New England tavern; its top made of one board is worn by centuries of hard use and scrubbing. In the foreground, the stern-looking portrait which could easily be mistaken for an American primitive, turns out to be just that, for it happens to be a portrait of a Dublin grandmother of the household, Lady Esther Dawson, painted on one of Lady Esther's long-ago visits.

In the east living room, on page 69, the subdued glow of golden and silvery tones in the woodwork demonstrates the loving attention of the craftsman. The first thing you will likely notice in here is the carved wooden chest of great antiquity, a German grain chest made in a day when such beautiful carving was done even on objects which were used in barns. Another rarity is the clay vase in the corner holding the dogwood, an Indian artifact, probably pre-Columbus and actually dug out of the earth near here, for this piece of country, still so untouched, abounds in Indian relics. The rocker, the most

*Dunstaffnage, at East Haddam: 1738–1790*

*The Lord House, in Essex: Late Eighteenth Century*

recent piece of furniture in the room, was one in which an ancestor of the household sat in 1799 while watching the funeral cortege of George Washington file by at the nation's capital.

The bedroom maintains the uncluttered simplicity of the rest of the house; the old maple bed without clutter or flounce, the log cabin–patterned quilt made in the neighborhood, the pine chest, might all have been used three centuries ago by the plain farm folk who lived here. The great central chimney provides, as here, a fireplace for every room in the house.

**D**UNSTAFFNAGE. Since the next house (page 67) belongs to an authority on early Connecticut architecture, it is not surprising to find it brilliantly executed.

In the living room, originally the kitchen, on page 70, the wide pine boards of both wall and ceiling, joined with feather edge and quarter-round molding, have been undisturbed since the house was built. Over the granite fireplace with its beehive brick bake-oven, sits an entirely original Erastus Hodges clock (collectors take note), rare Staffordshire plates, a pewter double-wick whale-oil lamp and candle sconces of eighteenth-century tinware. Facing into the room is a 1750 highboy of great dis-

tinction, claw-and-ball-footed with the original brasses. Arranged on top of it is more Staffordshire. To the left of this the comfortable-looking wing chair, of which only the front part is shown, was made in 1710, while the one in the foreground covered in a hand-blocked linen was made later in the century and is Chippendale.

The dining room, also on page 70, is a little breath-taking. Remodeled for a bride of the house in 1790, it makes a striking contrast to the living room. The style is, of course, a simplified Georgian and the fireplace with fluted cornerpost and casing, whose full entablature is crowned, is unique to East Haddam. The interesting piece on the mantel is a mirror portraying the Parthenon in miniature, which the owner has reason to believe was executed for Thomas Jefferson. The wonderful ocher color of the walls, with their crisp and delicious stencil decoration, was discovered under many coats of paint, now renewed so skillfully that you know it must look exactly as it did over two hundred and fifty years ago. The Empire sideboard is a Connecticut piece with matched mahogany veneer. Table and chairs were made in New York, traveled all the way to Holland with a bride, and were then returned again to this country. On the left of the fireplace stands an eighteenth-century ancestor of the Vic-

*The Mowings Dining Room*

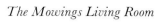

*A Mowings Bedroom*

69

*The Living Room in Dunstaffnage*

*The Dining Room in Dunstaffnage*

*The Lord House Dining Room*

torian whatnot, containing Sheffield platter covers and coffee urn.

LORD HOUSE. The elegance of the Lord house has been caught to perfection in this little dining room. Your eye will naturally be drawn to the cupboard, as indeed it should be, for it is a gem of delicate carving, paneled doors and butterfly shelves, painted to bring out the soap-bubble iridescence of the American blown-glass and pressed-glass collection, of which the rare early goblets on the table are a part.

The becoming deep-colored background of the figured wallpaper sets off the silver, the glass and particularly the Empire girandole over the mantel, a small jewel in its way too. The painting of the trim picks up a color in the paper, thus emphasizing the neat detail of the woodwork. The chairs are Chippendale type from Rhode Island. Draperies and china complete a gay, charming place.

*House of History, at Kinderhook: 1810*　　　　　*Home Sweet Home, at East Hampton: Late Seventeenth Century*

# The Diversity of New York State

### ROCK HALL, AT LAWRENCE; HOUSE OF HISTORY, AT KINDERHOOK;
### HOME SWEET HOME, AT EAST HAMPTON

IT would take more than the three houses here, or for that matter, more than any three New York houses you might select, to indicate the variety of early home-building styles in the state between the time of the simple ancient salt-box in East Hampton and that of the elegant Regency-like residence in Kinderhook. Could this be, we wonder, because the colonial and post-Revolutionary population of New York was so diverse? Remember, the polyglot character of the present population is by no means a recent development. As was pointed out in the chapter on Ethnic Groups in the excellent New York State Guide put out by the WPA, the colony, when it was still the New Netherland of the Dutch, already had representatives of a dozen other European nationalities. French-speaking Walloons were the first settlers of what is now Albany. As early as the seventeenth century there were Germans from the Palatinate; Norwegians, Danes, Scots, Irish and Welsh, all in considerable numbers. It is recorded that as early as 1644 eighteen different languages were being spoken. The English were

not only coming directly from England; they were coming from New England as well, to make the first settlements on the eastern end of Long Island. . . . It would take a good half-dozen houses to typify the wide variety of traditions and tastes, even before the Romantic Era opened. From the Greek Revival on, of course, no holds were any longer barred in architecture, and there was a bewilderment of styles, with New York State well in the lead. Up to then it was easy; and the houses were easy to look at, too—as these three houses show.

WHEN Rock Hall was new, the salt-meadow lands of Josiah Martin's farm swept in green waves of willows and grass almost from Jamaica Bay to the Atlantic Ocean. Now the mansion enjoys what is left of this landscape in a tiny park solidly surrounded by Lawrence, Long Island, in the Town of Hempstead, a matter of minutes from Manhattan. The colonial barns and outbuildings are gone, even their ghosts; but the great-house stands there in style, powder-white as a wig in this pretty protectorate of lawn and trees, filled to excitement with finery inside, and giving off its glow of Georgian elegance from pre-Revolutionary times. Rock Hall has the next thing to a one-family history; lived in only by Martins from 1767 to 1824, then only by Hewletts until 1948, when the Hewletts gave it to the Town of Hempstead, which maintains it now with polish and perfection for the pleasure of the public.

**B**UILT of tawny Hudson Valley brick when Kinderhook was a day-and-night journey by coach or schooner from New York, the House of History sits back from what was once the old stage road, and the river lies beyond. Others of the historic residential rivers, like the lower James with its stately brick Georgian mansions, and the winding Connecticut with its whiteness and redness of early wood-built homes, may be richer in certain single ways or manners of building, but none seems to us to tell as full a story of American houses as does the valley of the Hudson, with house after house of every period from pioneer Dutch dwellings to late Victorian villas of incredible luxuriance. And to our minds none of the old houses along the whole length of the Hudson from New York to Albany is better suited to represent the valley at its best than this fine example of the Regency fashion or Federal style which Barnabas Waterman designed and built at Kinderhook for a notable of the time named James Van der Poel, a New York judge. The house is aptly named, for it portrays the culture of the period and the culture of the valley in every detail of its design and decoration.

**N**ESTLED in verdure beside East Hampton's old village green, and watched over by one of Long Island's few remaining giant windmills, Home Sweet Home enjoys two claims to immortality: one as the boyhood home of John Howard Payne, whose celebrated song it must have certainly inspired, and the other as a living reminder of early colonial building methods so firm and true that after nearly three hundred years its only signs of age that really matter are the mellow beauties brought out by the passage of time. The men who put up this house and others like it in the locality were English settlers from New England, with plenty of oak at hand for framing, pine for paneling and cedar for shingling, and they used this wealth of woods for their New World homes in a way that was at once a tribute to their English training and the birth of a real American tradition in house design.

*Rock Hall, at Lawrence: 1767*

**R**OCK HALL. The rooms here have a freshness and animation about them as though their former occupants had just left them to pay a call. They achieve that rare combination of qualities: museum perfection and the lived-in look. They are all paneled, floor to ceiling; the wide panels in the downstairs rooms adding measurably to the distinguished proportions of a house whose scale is ample rather than manorial; the colors wonderfully pleasing throughout.

In the dining room, on page 74, with its fine American Chippendale, the rare delft pieces on the mantel and in the cupboard, together with the tiles, set the tone for the luxurious damask satin draperies and seat covers. The John Wollaston portrait, between the candlestick brackets with hurricane shades, and the lovely early mirror between the windows complete a flawless formal room.

The drawing room, on page 75, one of a pair furnished in the period of 1800 to 1810, as you can see from the mantel, is in the Federal style. The redecoration of these rooms was undertaken for a family wedding which must have been on the grand scale, for it was then that the rooms were thrown together with a wide arch between. New mantels and cornices, as well as new furniture, were some of the changes made for the great occasion. Perhaps the Martins, like a lot of us when we look at our old things in the light of a big party, felt that the parlors were simply not up-to-date and stylish enough in view of the throng of notables they were expecting.

The landscape over the fireplace was painted for the original panel in the eighteenth century, and fortunately the Martins decided to leave it there when they redecorated. The old harp, too, was a part of the gala scene and

*Rock Hall Dining Room*

the spinet with its lovely painted roses. Tables, chairs, mirrors and ornaments are of this later period, as is the unusually beautiful round Aubusson that adds so much to the refinement and richness of the room. It is a happy circumstance that the house presents us with two such becoming styles.

Back across the hall and back again to the eighteenth century, the parlor, on page 75, presided over by the striking young man in the bright red coat, has another distinguished mantel with the original tiles. The young man's identity is a mystery, but not that of the four Chippendale chairs, for we know they were bought for the house by the first family of Martins. The gaming table, with its old chess set, is English, and the needlework-embroidery fire screen is dated 1726.

Upstairs in Rock Hall there are four fine bedrooms like the one opposite, equally large, equally handsome, equally colorful. All in all, a house in a hundred.

HOUSE OF HISTORY. When you look at the rooms you will see that this house has great refinement of style. Over a carved Adamesque mantel in the parlor on page 76 is the portrait of Major Mordecai Myers, second owner of the house, who bought it from Judge Van der Poel and came there to live in 1836. The secretary, which is an eye-catcher, with its rare inlays of satinwood, is a most unusual piece of New York State Chippendale; while settee, wing chair, sewing and card tables were all made for Hudson Valley homes in Duncan Phyfe's shop about 1812. You will note the wide

*Rock Hall Drawing Room*

*A Rock Hall Bedroom*

*Rock Hall Parlor*

*House of History Drawing Room*

baseboard, paneled and reeded, and the carved medallions at the frame corners of the windows, which are so expertly draped; the ornaments too—candelabra, clock, Chinese tea jars, old dolls (a part of a large collection housed in another room)—are all of the choicest.

The dining room, opposite, casts an aura of muted brilliance. The panels of scenic Chinese wallpaper, the handsome pale-green damask draperies, the English china and silver, are admirable complements to the Duncan Phyfe dining set, made in 1814. But the most striking pieces of decoration are the window cornices, so delicately carved out of pine, and gilded, that you marvel they have survived intact.

If the Van der Poels furnished the house with the best contemporary things (and you may be sure they did), this is the way it would have looked—down to the handsomely carved Hudson Valley four-poster in the bedroom,

opposite, with its English chintz furnishings of the Regency Period, and its painted cornice. The polished oak floor is covered with priceless Persian scatter rugs.

HOME SWEET HOME. In the parlor (page 79) of what is now known as the Payne homestead, or Home Sweet Home (though the house was well over a hundred years old when the Paynes first occupied it), the ecclesiastical paneling was made by early ship carpenters. The furnishings are from several periods in the history of the house, and the portrait is of the poet Payne himself. The beautiful silver lusterware of which you see the pitchers, cups, saucers and crocus bowls on the mantel is only a fraction of an unusual collection of luster of every variety, which is displayed in the next room.

The kitchen (on page 78) is now, as it always was, the most important room in the house, well-equipped

*A House of History Bedroom*

*House of History Dining Room*

*Home Sweet Home Kitchen*

to play a many-purpose role, and clearly showing by the mammoth scale of the chimney alone what everlasting strength was built into these simple, unpretentious early dwellings. The rifles are hung as they would have been for easy reach, over the fireplace. Two ample ovens are built in the massive brick chimney, and the huge iron kettle hanging from a trivet, with smaller ones of copper nearby, will take care of the rest of the cookery. Please note the cooky cutters hanging on the wall and the neatly made spoon rack near them. Note, too, that ladles, wafer iron, and skillet have very long handles so that the cook will not scorch her hands when she moves the food to the fire.

The paneling becomes simpler upstairs, but the depth of the moldings, which pattern one whole wall of the bedroom, opposite, indicate the solidity of an entire house that would appear to have been built with eternity in mind. By contrast, the garnishing for all this solidity is fragile lusterware. More of it here on the mantel; the bowl, pitcher and chamber pot on the pretty commode are solid silver luster, too, making shimmers of brightness here and there in the quiet creams and browns of the room. The Sheraton-type four-poster that dates from the late eighteenth century, with its sober quilt from the neighborhood, the fine little Windsor armchair with bamboo turnings, complete this restful ambience.

*Home Sweet Home Parlor*

*Home Sweet Home Bedroom*

79

# The Pride of Pennsylvania

## POTTSGROVE, AT POTTSTOWN; WASHINGTON'S VALLEY FORGE HEADQUARTERS;
## THE MORRIS HOUSE, AT GERMANTOWN

JUST as the three distinguished old houses shown here have many features in common of style and construction, the early houses in the whole southeastern section of the state all bear unmistakable marks of resemblance. For one thing, as likely as not, outside walls are two feet through, and of most agreeable stone; and often between the rooms within, partitions are also apt to be of stone, and nearly as thick. Naturally, with all this weight and substance, there has been created right away one very strong regional characteristic. Sometimes perhaps it is pure simplicity; sometimes it is an exhibition of great style and sturdy sophistication; but always it is the strength and solidity that are the basic and dominant qualities. And these qualities, as is ever the case, were shared by the houses and the builders alike.

Take Pottsgrove, and its connection with the early ironmasters who did so much to develop this whole part of the country and create a new economy.

These men took the ore from the earth, and in their furnaces and forges turned it into usable iron—incidentally, of course, into the gold of great fortunes. The father of John Potts was among the foremost of these ironmasters, a Philadelphia Friend; and when John became head of the family on his father's death, and head of the family iron business, too, he was forty years old, married to a daughter of another famous ironmaster, and father of seven children (ultimately thirteen). That was in 1752.

He decided forthwith to build himself a suitable house, and this is it. It has the scale of a castle, the forthrightness of a farmhouse. Its simplicity befits a Quaker background, and gives nobility to its bigness and beauty. Among the great country houses of the large early landowners thereabouts, it was probably the best-looking and the largest. They were truly manorial, these houses; often far apart from each other because of the great extent of the holdings that surrounded them. Each manor had its workers' homes, its furnaces and forges, its springhouse, its grist mill, and its barns. And all with their walls laid up in this warm and wonderful Pennsylvania stone.

The front walls of the houses were often favored, as far as finish was concerned; and the front wall of Pottsgrove is a case in particular, for you can see the stone here is square-cut and laid up in range courses. The sidewall stone is square-cut, too, but the courses are random. Any square-cut job, whether laid up in range or in random courses, is called in Pennsylvania a "tailored stone wall," and is very special. Ordinarily, rubble masonry was the rule, in which the stone was laid up rough as it comes from the quarry.

Another example of tailored stone is fifteen miles away from Pottsgrove toward Philadelphia, where John Potts' fourth son, Isaac, an ironmaster, too, lived in a house that became forever famous in the winter of 1777 as Washington's Valley Forge Headquarters. This house is quite a lot smaller than Pottsgrove; in fact, it was a pretty tight squeeze for Washington and his entourage; so tight that the General caused a log cabin to be built out back to serve as a dining room for him and his numerous staff; it being his custom to have his meals always with the officers and friends who worked closely with him in the field.

On the evening before the General's birthday in 1778, Martha Washington came to join her husband in the house which he had occupied since Christmas. They stayed together here until June, during the most desperate days of the Revolution, sustaining the courage of the ragged and suffering army. After their departure, the Potts family, who had taken temporary quarters nearby, duly returned to their home, and lived on there for many years with a new sense of pride in their house. Now it is visited every year by a quarter of a million people, who are able to enjoy it as much for its livable and substantial beauty as for the part it played in our country's past.

The three houses that speak here for Pennsylvania have all by coincidence been closely connected with the Father of his Country. It was at Pottsgrove that the General made his headquarters between the battles of Brandywine and Germantown for five days in September 1777, three months or so before his occupation of Valley Forge; and it was in what we now call the Morris House that he lived briefly sixteen years later while President.

This house was built by a wealthy Philadelphian named David Deschler, quite a colorful character, and a dabbler in pharmacy, who invented a salve that is still being sold under his name. It is believed that he was in the house when in the fog of October 4, 1777, it began to look as though our weary men were winning the battle of Germantown. The redcoats were retreating. Then from out of the mist, fresh British reinforcements burst into view; and that was that.

Almost at once this was the house that caught the eye of Sir William Howe. Nearly new, nicely furnished, and right on the Market Square, it made handsome headquarters for the English commander's last winter in America.

Deschler had died, and the house was owned by a man named Franks when the discriminating eye of Washington himself was caught by its attractions. He lived in it during November 1793, and in it he spent most of the following summer. Several mornings a week he would ride into the capital, which was then Philadelphia, returning with relief from the hot afternoons of that city to the stone-cool comfort of this great good-looking country-town mansion. It was the center of that summer's excitement, for not only were all the fine figures of the

*The Morris House, at Germantown: 1772*

*Washington's Valley Forge Headquarters: 1758*

young republic to be seen coming and going, but it was the summer when Martha Washington did her own marketing in the Square. Ever since, it has led a comparatively uneventful life; beautifully lived in by succeeding families of Morrises from 1834 until it was given by the Morrises to the United States as a national shrine, maintained by the Germantown Historical Society.

*A Pottsgrove Bedroom*

*The Pottsgrove Dining Room*

*Children's Dining Room at Pottsgrove*

VALLEY FORGE. The rooms in Quaker John Potts' house were not large, but there were plenty of them, and their appointments were of the best. Mr. Potts observed the principles of simplicity which his convictions enjoined. The lack of ornament notwithstanding, his house was built extravagantly well when it came to workmanship and materials. One concession to elegance in the parlor is the marble facing of the fireplace. The massive walnut desk contains the inlaid initials "I. P." and was made in 1775. Above the Pennsylvania stretcher table with drop-leaf ends hangs an early American panel portrait, chairs are Philadelphia Chippendale. A typical Revolutionary hat, cloak and saber can be seen hanging on the wall through the arched doorway.

The dining room became the General's office, its gate-leg table now holding his diary, his wooden inkwell, a pair of Sheffield candlesticks and a brass telescope. The armchair is Pennsylvania wainscot, while over the mantel, with its Queen Anne side brackets, hangs a contemporary black-and-white print of Philadelphia.

In Martha's bedroom with its fishnet-canopied four-poster, was a daily gathering of officers' wives and neighboring farm women who spent hours patching uniforms, darning stockings, knitting outfits, and preparing food and medicine for the many ailing soldiers. The mahogany chest of drawers is Chippendale; the toile de Jouy quilted spread, like most of the furnishings, predates Washington's occupancy. A ladder-back dressing chair and armchair, bed warmer and candlesticks complete the early comforts afforded to the First Lady during the hard winter of '78.

The brick-floored kitchen is dominated by the huge fireplace, holding the necessary wrought-iron and copper utensils of the time—the skillets, kettles, tongs, trammel, wafer irons, candle molds, fruit press, and of course, the Paul Revere lantern on the left. Besides, there are the pewter dishes and porringers ranged on the sideboard, and the rare pewter oblong fish plate with octagonal edges on the mantel. Hickory kitchen chairs with delicate spindles emphasize the sturdiness of the sawbuck table and sideboard.

*Headquarters Parlor*

*A Headquarters Bedroom*

*Headquarters Office*

*Headquarters Kitchen*

*A Morris House Bedroom*

*The Morris House Drawing Room*

THE MORRIS HOUSE. The sharp definition of the moldings, the mantelpieces that state their excellence without ostentation and the recessed windows with their twenty-four panes typify the fine houses in the vicinity of Philadelphia which were built in these early days by prosperous but sober merchants like David Deschler who built this one.

The colors were apt to be quite gay. Here in these rooms the original paint has been followed as closely as possible. The drawing room, whose colors are most pleasing with its dark ribbon of blue around the baseboard and the blue marble chimney facing, has a wonderful portrait over the mantel of the Washington family just as it was during the relaxed Germantown sojourn—George and Martha with the Custis grandchildren whom they had adopted and adored—suggesting in its setting that it might have been painted right here that summer.

The handsome secretary desk is a New England piece of the period; the Venetian blinds are the original ones of the house.

While this is the bedroom in which Washington slept, the big fourposter is not the one in which he slept during his sojourns at the Morris house, though it is more nearly his size than many a bed in which the President did sleep. The bedroom across the hall was Martha's.

In the dining room the shield-back Hepplewhite chairs belonged to the Morris family, and the distinguished Hepplewhite cabinet, with its circular inlays of wreaths and eagles, was made about 1760. The table is a rope-leg Sheraton. The set of export china was one that was used by the Washingtons, for which the inventory shows that not a single piece was chipped when the house was returned to its owner. The silver tea set is one that belonged to Alexander Hamilton.

*The Morris House Dining Room*

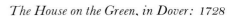
*The House on the Green, in Dover: 1728*

# *Distinction in Delaware*

## ASPENDALE, AT DOWNS CHAPEL;

## THE HOUSE ON THE GREEN, IN DOVER

THE eye is caught in this little state by the early brick houses that decorate it, town and country. Of the country houses, Aspendale happens to be a notable example, but there are many others to be seen that can make driving a delight; and there are many houses clustered in certain of the towns that by the same token can make stopping a pleasure not to be missed. Yet it can be shown that a million people a year, speeding past on one of the principal north-south highways of the nation, miss the town of New Castle by a matter of yards—a town illustrated in the first *Treasury*, and as treasurable an early American town as any in the country. Then farther down there is Odessa, in which a delightful part to see, off to one side, is still in a deep colonial dream. And finally in Dover you arrive at a very choice rectangle of grass and trees in the ancient center of the town, laid out just as William Penn had directed. And just as he knew it would, this little green square has attracted a border about it of one beautiful old brick house after another, of which the one called here the House on the Green is an outstanding beauty. Flush on the sidewalk, and faced in Flemish bond, it is furnished, as will be seen, with the affection that only a house receives which has been in the family for two hundred years.

ASPENDALE. The interior of Aspendale has modest manners which belie its rare character. It does not call attention; on the contrary, it discloses itself very sub-

*Aspendale, at Downs Chapel: 1771*

tly. The longer you look at these rooms, the more you become aware of their qualities.

The owner, who cherishes his house as his ancestor who built it obviously did, has devoted much time and thought to its restoration. The furniture, like the house itself, is fine and simple. It is used with restraint and you can be sure these interiors never were and never will be crowded. Each piece is just right for its place in the house, the Windsors and ladder-backs, the early cherry four-poster with its chaste canopy and homespun cover, seem to partake of the timeless quality of their setting. So much has never been changed here. By some great good fortune even the paint on the plaster walls and woodwork is the original first and only coat, brushed on in 1771! As you see, every room has paneling which gave the ingenious painter a wide scope for his fascinating color combinations. On the woodwork, wonderful tones of gray, brown and green are used. The drawing room shown on page 91 is a bluish green which would be hard to match. Some of the other combinations used are strawberry pink and gray, wistaria and deep olive green, light grape and brown.

*The Aspendale Library*

*The Aspendale Dining Room*

*An Upstairs Hallway in Aspendale*

Each room is elegantly proportioned, each has its own fireplace, even the cozy upstairs hall, as you can see, with its perfect little bannister. There are no mantelpieces in the house and all of the fireplaces are finished in moldings, the result being restrained and immensely stylish. In almost every room there are balancing cupboards on either side of the fireplaces, the doors still fitting perfectly into the paneling. Windows are unusually spacious, filling the house with light.

To come upon this simple third-floor bedroom, shown opposite, with its own unusually small fireplace (opening twelve by twelve inches), and its unusually large chimney breast, is almost like a playful afterthought of someone who is pointing up the delicious effects that may also be achieved through disproportion. You will notice that all the fireside baskets are filled with twigs rather than kindling wood, characteristic of the many little thoughtful touches the owner bestows upon this most satisfying house.

THE HOUSE ON THE GREEN. This room (page 92), with its books and comfort, is, in the plan of the house, a hall, yet it has been lived in as much as any room in the house. Its central position, its big sunny windows, its paneling dark with age, give it an irresistible quality of warmth and welcome. The stairs, floors, wainscot and trim are all the original pine and cedar built into the house some 225 years ago. Since almost everything in the house has been in the Ridgeley family for many

*The Aspendale Living Room*

*A Third-Floor Fireplace in Aspendale*

*An Aspendale Bedroom*

generations, it will be unnecessary to say so again in describing these two rooms. The sofa, back to the bay window, is eighteenth-century Philadelphia Chippendale, and the two chairs in the extreme foreground are also Philadelphia. The Queen Anne tea table is set with Orange Peel Lowestoft, given by General Anthony Wayne to Mary Vining, a Revolutionary belle, whose several portraits show her to have been one of the great beauties of that or any other era. Before you leave this comfortable room, note the fireback, marked "Batso Foundry" and made about 1750.

The hall opens into the formal parlor which contains a great number of the family treasures with which this house abounds. The room has the quality of a jewel box. Over the charming mantel is a portrait of Mary Wyncoop Ridgeley, painted by Charles Willson Peale in 1773. The French porcelain urns at either end of the mantel were a wedding gift of the Cadwalader cousins from Philadelphia in 1803. The small pictures you see are eighteenth-century prints by Cipriani of Padua. The exquisite draperies were hand-loomed.

*The Dover House Drawing Room*

*The Dover House Hallway-Library*

*Cremona, in St. Marys County: 1819*

# The Maryland Manner

## CREMONA, IN ST. MARYS COUNTY; TULIP HILL, IN ANNE ARUNDEL;

## BOSTON CLIFF AND TROTH'S FORTUNE, IN TALBOT

FROM the time of Troth's Fortune to the time of Cremona, Maryland houses went up in the various ways that were successively customary as a century and a half wore on from early colonial to early republican years. The forms are familiar. The early simplicity of steeply gabled or gambreled roofs, great chimneys; then the elegance and stateliness of the Georgian, both before and after the Revolution, and finally the refined solidity of the Federal—all at least touched upon here, as it happens, in these four houses. The forms, the styles, were common to houses elsewhere, or reasonably so. What was outstanding about Maryland

houses was their *stylishness*. It was something beyond excellence. It was a certain manner, presence, air. It was something that might have come from having made a particular point to be attractive.

The Maryland builders did beautiful things with brick from the very beginning, and they had plenty of practice. For early Maryland houses are as numerous as they are hard for a stranger to find without guidance. In Henry C. Forman's *Early Manor and Plantation Houses of Maryland*, well over five hundred houses from before 1800 are given scholarly consideration. And the author speaks casually, as a native who knows his way through the tidewater trails, of having made a personal survey of fifteen hundred. Writing as of 1934, he estimates that of the twenty-five to fifty thousand houses of Colonial Maryland, five thousand remain.

The early houses of Maryland are also noted for their picturesque names. There is an Adam's Adventure, a Brother's Content; there was a Clean Drinking Manor that is now destroyed. Hockley-in-the-Hole is one; My Lord's Gift another; and a Talbot County neighbor of Troth's Fortune and Boston Cliff is one called Crooked Intention.

Maryland is a state in which the counties carry as much individual identity and importance as the states do in the nation, if not more. Architectural historians describe the early houses in terms of the counties in which the houses stand, and point out the building methods and mannerisms peculiar to that county. When you take part in Maryland's famous annual house and garden pilgrimage, one day is devoted to each county, and each county is individually organized to guide and entertain you.

The county in which Cremona stands is St. Marys in Southern Maryland. The county was "erected," as they say, in 1637, named after the Virgin Mary and contained in it the city of St. Mary, the first capital of the province. As for Cremona itself, on page 93, standing under its towering willow oaks beside the Patuxent, here you have Maryland at its mellowest. One of the later of the great early country houses, it has the distinctiveness of the Maryland manner as you approach it, and as you enter it, one of the country's most extraordinary staircases, a hanging double stairway that fills the great hall like a modern abstraction.

Anne Arundel is the county of Annapolis, the Severn, and of the house called Tulip Hill—one of Maryland's very best, standing in a grove of ancient tulip poplars and on a lovely rise of land which together gave the house its

*A Cremona Bedroom*

name. It is a fortunate house as great houses go. Beautiful to begin with, it has had no disasters, no disfigurements. And now, nearing its two-hundredth birthday, it finds itself in the hands of discerning and devoted owners able to lavish it with attentions.

It was built by Samuel and Anne Galloway, wealthy Quakers; but it was never to be lived in by them together, Anne dying in childbed just before the house was ready.

*Tulip Hill, in Anne Arundel County: 1756*

*The Tulip Hill Dining Room*

*The Tulip Hill Drawing Room*

*The Tulip Hill Hallway*

And although there is a Cupid carved in the pediment of the porch, Samuel never remarried. He prospered in the foreign trade with his fleet of ships; among them the *Tulip*, the *Grove*, the *Planter*, the *Swallow*. He established a famous stable of racing horses, and entertained tremendously at Tulip Hill. George Washington dropping in for dinner before a ball or after the races was a matter of common occurrence—if anything that happened then and there can be looked upon now as a common occurrence—either the people, their place in history, or the wonderful old houses themselves.

Many of the furnishings in the fine old house betoken the present owners' long residence in China, from where so much of the eighteenth-century English decoration received its inspiration, making the Queen Anne and Sheraton you see here much at home with the rare Chinese objects. As you enter, the glories of the broad entrance hall begin with the double pendent arch, considered one of the unique features of this house. But you see first the wide shell-crowned cupboard with its butterfly shelves, a thing which almost takes your breath away with its exquisite collection of milk-glazed blanc de chine, translucent ware that served as a model for most of the early European porcelains. The filtered light of the hall, playing on this whole lovely thing, creates a rosy iridescence like an afterglow.

To the right of the hall, the drawing room is dominated by a magnificent Chinese screen which is composed

*Boston Cliff, in Talbot County: Early Eighteenth Century*

of scrolls hand-painted on silk, depicting a festivity in the tea garden of a great mandarin more than 250 years ago. The bronze goose in the foreground is an incense burner; in the background through the lighted doorway is a graceful woodcarving of Kwan Yin. On the mantel are rare Peking enamels. At the left of the fireplace is a mahogany and satinwood Sheraton armchair, at the right a Queen Anne walnut settee, both looking thoroughly at home with the chinoiserie.

Back through the double arch of the hallway to the left is the dining room (page 96); smaller scale than the rest of the house. Here on the graceful Adam mantel are more Chinese porcelain plates, the "Ten Colour" ware, favorite of the Manchus, their brilliant coral hue repeated almost exactly in the color of the japonica bouquet on the Sheraton dining table. Chairs are Hepplewhite. Standing on either end of the bow-front Sheraton sideboard are jewel trees with jade leaves and carnelian cherries, and over it hangs a wonderful Japanese screen of gold paper painted in what is called the Chinese style, its colors wonderfully mellowed by age.

TALBOT COUNTY is on the Eastern Shore, which is a tidewater paradise of large and little creeks and rivers creeping in and out of the Chesapeake. And it is near the banks of these countless estuaries that the finest early houses are to be found; for when they were built, the best way to reach them was by water, and still is in some cases. These two small and early manor houses are extremely choice, even for Talbot County. They are near the Choptank, and are known as the North Choptank type, with high gables, low eaves, deli-

cate dormers, impressive chimneys, and colorful names.

The color of old Maryland brick has to be seen to be believed, but here at Boston Cliff you get a good idea of how beautiful it is. On the plaster of one of the chimneys, someone has scratched the date of 1729, but the house may well be older than that, the land having been surveyed in 1663.

The house built in the seventeenth century by William Troth has the same beautiful brick as Boston Cliff. Even with a gambrel roof instead of a straight gable, the family resemblance between these two neighboring North Choptank houses is remarkable. It is too bad that both faces of a house can't appear in the same picture, for on the other front of Troth's Fortune an interesting feature of an almost medieval nature is the engaged staircase tower, rising like a semi-separate part of the house, and betraying its great age and medieval nature.

Its living room is one that is remembered with special delight. Its paneling is full of grace, set off now by its subtle coloring. The room is neither perfectionist nor precious, but it is as nearly radiant as a room can be.

In the "great rooms" of these two houses, the similarities in the architectural detailing of the paneled fireplace walls might easily be missed because of the differences. The Boston Cliff drawing room (page 100) is done in the direction of brilliance and formality; the living room at Troth's Fortune stays quiet and casual by comparison.

The paneling in both is the ancient original yellow pine that was put in considerably over two hundred years

*Troth's Fortune, in Talbot County: Late Seventeenth Century*

*The Troth's Fortune Living Room*

ago and probably painted, as was the custom then. The window seats in both rooms, likewise paneled, are a charming and unusual feature of this section. In fact, from fluted pilasters framing arched fireplaces, to the high paneled dado and the sturdy cornices, these houses are country manors on a small scale, beautifully finished to suit their position in the neighborhood back in the eighteenth century—when they stood in the thinly populated country as the impressive abodes of the local squirearchy.

The furniture in the parlor of Boston Cliff is eighteenth-century English and American. The Queen Anne walnut secretary with mirrors and the Chippendale open-arm chair in the foreground are Philadelphia pieces. The dainty pair of commodes that stand for incidental tables

now are Queen Anne. The portraits, both here and over the dining-room mantel are of Virginia ancestors of the present owners.

The dining room, page 100, where the color of the mantel picks up the red in the portrait, is plainer, but the paneled dado and window seats persist. The open-beamed ceiling extends the full width of the house. The mantel is intricately detailed with a nice bolection molding for finish, and on either end of it are some fine early Sheffield candlesticks with oval globes. Lowestoft plates complete the garniture. The Hepplewhite bow-front sideboard is an English beauty of the eighteenth century, as is the mirror above it. The glasses on the Duncan Phyfe table are Waterford; chairs Chippendale.

*The Boston Cliff*
*Dining Room*

*The Boston Cliff*
*Drawing Room*

# District of Columbia

## DUMBARTON HOUSE, ON Q STREET; THE LINDENS, ON KALORAMA ROAD

WHILE the city of Washington, as created by the first President from sections of land contributed by Maryland and Virginia totaling one hundred square miles, contained at first both Alexandria and Georgetown, it now contains only the latter; Alexandria having managed to tear itself loose in 1846 and return to Virginia. Had Alexandria stayed in, the residents of the District, who have no voice in their local government, no representation in Congress, and no vote for President, could at least have boasted having more fine early American homes than any city in the nation. For both Georgetown and Alexandria are replete; together, no other city could touch them. As it is, Georgetown now provides the bulk of the District's best early houses, of which Dumbarton is an exceptional specimen. The Lindens is an earlier house, but a very recent arrival here, having been brought down from Danvers, Massachusetts, in the 1930's.

Dumbarton was named Bellevue when it was built, and there are those who feel that its name should never have been changed; though with a large city crowding in around it, the beautiful prospect to which its original name referred has now only its historical significance. But as everyone agrees who visits there, the house itself is a beautiful sight, which is all that really matters any more.

Then there are people who feel that The Lindens should really be known as the General Gage house. For when the British commander in 1774 had been commissioned Governor of Massachusetts to put down our patriotic outbursts—to no avail (merely bringing on the Revolution)—he made The Lindens his residence. This house had been built in Danvers as the summer home of the Honorable Robert Hooper, a great man of Marblehead, called "King" Hooper by the fishermen there. His Marblehead house was one of the showpieces of that town, and still is today.

The Lindens was named from a grove of these trees that grew around it in Danvers, and it has been reported that while the house is now gone, the lindens remain, and the place name too. But the house is a great house, whatever it is called, or wherever it is taken. It is a masterpiece of colonial carpentry, with a gambrel, balustraded roof, and an entrance motif two-and-a-half stories high, with pediment and pilasters. Its front siding is grooved and then sanded to resemble ashlar-cut masonry, like Mount Vernon down the Potomac, and like the Lee mansion back in our Massachusetts pages—where The Lindens might have been.

*Dumbarton House, on Q Street: Early Nineteenth Century*

*The Lindens, on Kalorama Road: 1754*

Dumbarton Music Room
Over the mantel is a charming portrait of the children of Samuel Washington, and at the window end of the room you can see a carved gilt console with marble top, and between the richly draped windows an ornate Adam mirror.

Dumbarton Dining-Room Mantel

DUMBARTON HOUSE. The rooms of Dumbarton House sparkle; the setting, of course, is Adam. What else could give it all this graceful elegance and charm? The delicacy and lightness of the mantels in the parlor, and particularly in the dining room, set the style for the whole décor.

Besides the mantel, the blue parlor has many little refinements of molding, chair rail and cornice. This room opens into the oval music room, most of which you will have to look at, in this picture, through the strings of a harp. Look up above it, too, for there depends from the ceiling another example of the art of the fabricator of domestic accessories in those days—a sapphire glass chandelier made in Russia in the eighteenth century.

*A Dumbarton Bedroom*
*This bedroom could not be more lusciously and purely feminine, from its white embroidered bedspread and canopied Sheraton field bed to its Leeds luster-covered jars on the mantelpiece presumably for rose leaves, vervain or lavender.*

*The Dumbarton Drawing Room*
*The pretty Sheraton desk with oval mirrors, made of mahogany and satinwood, the exquisitely inlaid Pembroke tea table with twin chairs, on which the cabinetmaker has also lavished his skill in the special art of inlay, all of these pieces suit their setting perfectly.*

*The outstanding feature of the house is the stairway with its woodwork and hand-blocked French wallpapers, making the hallway, as an authority has stated, one of the three finest in the country.*

*The dining-room chairs (opposite, lower right) are wonderful examples of New York State craftsmanship, slat-back Chippendale, claw-and-ball-footed.*

*What makes the bedroom (below) the most important of the four immense ones on the paneled second floor is the fabulous English crewelwork which furnishes both bed and window draperies, embroidered in the early times of Charles II, and beyond price.*

*The Lindens Stair Hall*

THE LINDENS. Since the extraordinary interiors of this great house are of museum perfection, perhaps it is in order to say that the owner of the house is a gifted antiquarian whose unstinted time and effort have produced something of a masterpiece of re-creation. In the house everything is mid-eighteenth century. To quote the owner, "not even the design for a curtain valance is later than 1754."

The drawing room, on the left of the hall as you enter, is pilastered and paneled from floor to ceiling, its scale so just that you are hardly aware of its size. The furniture, Queen Anne and Chippendale, is entirely of the mid-century period of the house; the prize, perhaps, the noble American sofa with its fine form and heroic proportions.

*The Lindens Drawing Room*

*The Lindens Dining Room*

*The Crewel Bedroom
in The Lindens*

*Kenmore, at Fredericksburg: 1752*

# Vintage Virginia

WILTON, AT RICHMOND; KENMORE, AT FREDERICKSBURG; THE BRUSH-EVERARD HOUSE
AND THE NICOLSON HOUSE, AT WILLIAMSBURG; THE MOORE HOUSE, AT YORKTOWN

IN its new home on a terraced hilltop high above the James, Wilton's noble features plainly place it in the great American mid-Georgian tradition. While it was being carried here piece by piece from certain destruction six miles away, and being marvelously put together again where you see it now on the outskirts of Richmond, a present-day workman discovered underneath a section of bedroom molding a penciled message from the past: "Sampson Darrell put up this cornish in the year of our Lord 1753." So, although the dates of great houses are often disputed, the Wilton date was settled then and there. It was built by William Randolph III, and practically every person of pre-Revolutionary importance was a friend of the family and a frequent guest in the house. Every room, from baseboard to "cornish," is completely paneled, even to the closets or alcoves that flank all eight big chimney breasts—putting Wilton in a class by itself.

AT two times in its career it was touch and go with Kenmore. The first was about twenty-five years after Colonel Fielding Lewis had built it for his bride Betty, the only sister of George Washington.

In the operation of the revolutionary gunnery at Fredericksburg he exhausted his personal fortune, with the result that after his death the property was held for taxes. It was Washington who then saved the house for his sister. And until 1922 it managed quite well under various owners. At this point, two Fredericksburg women with extraordinary spirit and enterprise organized a group of local ladies, who not only saved the house from much worse than a tax sale, but gathered sufficient funds from far and wide to effect its beautiful restoration.

AT WILLIAMSBURG, you come to the Palace Green and turn in toward the Palace. Then you come to a little house half hidden behind the crape myrtles. Like a lot of early eighteenth-century houses, this one, too, is larger than it looks. The John Brush who began it in 1717 gave the house its outward air of modesty. It was Thomas Everard who, being a mansion-type man, and becoming its owner in the mid-1700's, commanded its almost mansion-like interiors. The kitchen, the office and other dependencies make the whole place a gentleman's establishment, small, complete and polished.

*The Moore House, at Yorktown: Early Eighteenth Century*

*The Brush-Everard House, at Williamsburg: 1717*

*Wilton, at Richmond: 1753*

THE NICOLSON HOUSE is not a part of the stunning colonial exhibition town of Williamsburg, but stands a few steps out York Street from where the restoration starts, on what looks a lot like many another small-town street in Virginia today. It was the home in 1766 of Robert Nicolson, a prominent townsman and tailor of Williamsburg, for that was the year he advertised "genteel lodgings" there with breakfast and good stabling for "gentlemen who attend the General Courts and Assembly." As good as saying that almost anyone who was anyone in colonial times could have stopped here, especially if the Raleigh Tavern had been full.

A DOZEN or more miles away from Williamsburg, and close by the battleground of Yorktown, is one of the most engaging houses in Virginia. It gets its name from the Augustine Moores who bought it in 1768. The big day for this beautiful house was October 18, 1781— an even bigger day for the nation. At two o'clock that afternoon there arrived by arrangement Colonel John Laurens and the Vicomte de Noailles, representing the American and French allies, and a few minutes later Lieutenant Colonel Thomas Dundas and Major Alexander Ross, representing the British. When the four men left the house that evening, fourteen articles of capitulation had been drawn up and agreed upon. It only remained for General Washington to approve. As for the house, it now belongs to the people of this country—a house of which any one of us would approve.

*The Nicolson House, at Williamsburg: 1750's*

*The Northwest Drawing Room at Wilton*

WILTON. Unique among the great Queen Anne mansions of Virginia, which can lay claim to some of the finest, is Wilton, whose eight stately rooms and two immense halls are paneled floor to ceiling, including even the closets on either side of the fireplaces in each room. All of this fine woodwork, with the exception of the walnut stairway, is pine. In the important rooms of the period all such paneling was painted. The colors here are as close to the originals as experts could make them. There are no mantelpieces in the house, but every fireplace has a marble facing and hearth, six of which are the originals, as are the hardware and locks with few exceptions.

Over the mantel in the library is a copy of the striking portrait of Washington by Peale. The oxbow chest of drawers between the windows sits under a fine Queen Anne mirror of unusual length crowned with a mask and

Prince of Wales feathers. The two small Hepplewhite shield-back chairs at the table were made in Norfolk. Warm colors and patterns in the Turkish rug make this an inviting room for reading, gaming or intimate conversations.

The first things you see in the nursery, a room bright with sunlight and airily draped in white, are the beds—one a child's Sheraton field bed, and the other a baby's Hepplewhite field crib—whose cobweb canopies of tied thread add to the gauzy enchantment here. The spreads are blue and white hand-woven coverlets. At the window is an arrow-back high chair for baby, and by the crib a slat-back armchair for nurse. In one of the window-lighted closets of this evocative room, is a steep concealed staircase which leads down to the mother's chamber so that she may get to the nursery instantly without having to make the long trip around in the great hallway.

*A Child's Bedroom at Wilton*

*The Northeast Drawing Room at Wilton*

*The Drawing Room at Kenmore*

KENMORE. This beautifully restored mansion today is much as it must have been when the Lewises lived there, antedating the great events which were "to bring forth a nation." The echoes of our history can be heard in every room.

The drawing room is dominated by the "Four Horns of Plenty" ceiling, aided and abetted by the plaster over-mantel plaque whose design was suggested by Washington, which depicts an Aesop Fable called "The Fox, The Crow and The Piece of Cheese." This was meant as a very decorative lesson to the Lewis children to beware of flattery. These tours de force of intricate and exquisite plaster-work were executed by talented Hessian prisoners of war.

Most of the furniture in the room is fine Chippendale, the two fireside chairs original possessions of Charles Washington, the General's youngest brother. Delft ornaments and chinoiserie are the garniture, as well as many other appointments. The beautiful chandelier was made in 1760; and the Turkish carpet is a very rare Oushak.

In the dining room with its somewhat more restrained ornamentation, the carving under the mantel is the Washington crest, "The Swan and the Crown." The hunting board, of which you see part, was originally owned by Mary Washington, and the triple silver urn on it was a Lewis possession. The portrait of Colonel Fielding Lewis, which is companioned by one of his wife, Betty, on the

*A Bedroom at Kenmore*

*The Brush-Everard Downstairs Bedroom*

other side of the Chippendale wall clock made by Storr of London, was painted as a gift for Lawrence Lewis and Nellie Custis, his wife.

Upstairs the guest rooms were always occupied; the Washingtons, the Lewises and their friends were forever coming and going. All the bedrooms are delightful, but the one shown here, belonging to Mistress Betty, is perhaps the prettiest and certainly the most feminine. The fresh pink walls are outlined by a pale blue cornice, the blue repeated in delft jars on the mantel, in the rare Persian prayer carpets on the floor and in the old toile bedhangings and cover. The four-poster itself belonged to Betty. It was on this very bed that she found her brother

George, who had flung himself there exhausted, when he returned from the battle at Yorktown, too tired to announce his arrival. There he slept in his muddy boots, in all the feminine finery. At the foot of the bed is Betty's little traveling trunk, and at the head a dainty tripod washstand with its decorated bowl and ewer.

THE BRUSH-EVERARD HOUSE. You are struck at once by a sophistication in the furnishing that the simplicity of the exterior has hardly led you to expect, and a stunning brilliance of color. The rooms are not large but the scale is perfect, a thing you are likely to take for granted in Williamsburg. The mid-eighteenth-century English

*The Brush-Everard Parlor*

landscape by an unknown artist fits the overmantel as perfectly as do all the other furnishings in Mr. Everard's parlor. On the tripod mahogany tea table the gay dishes are Chinese export porcelain (1750–60). The chairs are Chippendale. In a room whose furnishings are in some instances unique, perhaps most striking are the hangings and upholstery of red watered moreen, a woolen material whose brilliance two centuries has failed to dim. It comes from another Virginia plantation nearby and its condition is little short of a miracle, part of the secret being that wool tends to hold its color better than other fabrics. The portrait of the little woman in pink is of Mrs. Elizabeth Stith, by William Dering, dated 1763.

Everything in the northeast blue bedroom downstairs is eighteenth-century and here again it is the color that first seizes you. Right up in the foreground the red chair is Chippendale, as is the chest at the other end of the room, surmounted by a Queen Anne walnut mirror. Next to it stands a charming tripod wash-stand which contains a marked Worcester basin and a Bristol delft ewer. The lovely needlework picture over the simple mantel is dated 1763. The five-piece garniture is probably English china. The blue-patterned wallpaper was reproduced from fragments of the original found under the cornices when the house was being restored. It can be purchased now at the Craft Shop, up the street.

*The Nicolson Library*

THE NICOLSON HOUSE. It is clear that the owner of this house is a connoisseur and collector of eighteenth-century American and English furniture and expert at recreating a house of the period, having had much to do with furnishing the Wythe House in the Williamsburg restoration proper, pictured in the first *Treasury*. The house therefore contains many choice pieces, the result of lifetime collecting in many places.

Perhaps the most exciting of these three rooms is the dining room with its light fruitwoods. The sideboard of applewood was found in South Carolina, and the delightful painting over it is the owner's great grandmother. The knife boxes at each end were made from a Chinese camphor chest. The polished copper urn and tray, the copper candlesticks, are English about 1780. Copper rather than silver helps this room to glow with a subdued brilliance.

The dining table is applewood from North Carolina and the side chairs are English fruitwood from Yorkshire. The narrow corner cupboard is pine and like the table contains old Canton blue and white china. The red draperies of raw silk, the soft blue paneling, are a perfect background for this symphony of woods.

The parlor here is more formal with its sturdy dentiled cornice and its simple corner mantel and English brass fireplace fittings. The painting which so admirably fits the overmantel is also English of the period. The sofa, the tea table in front of it, the leather armchair, the armchair in the foreground and the yellow upholstered side chair are all mahogany, all English Chippendale. The rug is a fine Oriental whose red is a foil for the bright yellows and paler greens in the room, a combination of colors by an accomplished hand. The most unusual feature of this room is the

*The Nicolson Drawing Room*

*The Nicolson Dining Room*

*The Moore Dining Room*

original molding which divides the plaster walls, said to be a picture molding. This room opens into a small library, also paneled, which offers a snug retreat from the rest of the house, with its Connecticut clock on the mantel.

The colors throughout the house are copied exactly from the original coats of paint found in it.

MOORE HOUSE. The drawing room, where the articles of capitulation were finally drawn up, shows a forthright countrified solidity in mantel, deeply molded chair rail and heavily mullioned windows. Next to the mantel stands a rare mahogany dumbwaiter (1750–75). The daintily decorated china on it is Chelsea ware. The splat-back Chippendale armchair pulled up to the circular mahogany table might easily have been the place where Colonel John Laurens sat in the conference. The fine portrait by Girolamo Batoni completes the re-

creation of this small room whose walls have witnessed such significant events in our history.

The dining-room mantel, eloquent of the period and locale, is enhanced by pewter and a portrait in oils of Alexander Fraser by Jeremiah Theus. To the right of the fireplace is a walnut cellaret, while the mahogany dining table, set for the conferees to refresh themselves during their long deliberations, is eighteenth-century Chippendale, the chairs Chippendale likewise.

The bedroom with its little corner fireplace, seen through the gracefully canopied field bed, with bare pine floor and recessed dormers, makes plain the simple homeliness which is the character of this house. The bed quilt of local make and pattern dominates all. But the high and low chests, both of walnut and Chippendale in style, hold their own anywhere, as does the perfect Windsor by the fireside.

*A Bedroom in the Moore House*

*A Parlor in the Moore House*

# In the Tidewater Carolinas

TWO HOUSES IN NEW BERN; A PLANTATION HOUSE ON EDISTO;

AND SIX OF CHARLESTON'S FINEST DRAWING ROOMS

NOW in New Bern you will begin to notice what a Philadelphian named William Attmore noticed in 1787 in writing about that enchanting town. "There are to many of the houses," he said, "Balconies or Piazzas in front and sometime back of the house, this Method of Building is found convenient on account of the great Summer Heats here." For from here on down, these appendages, whether called balconies or piazzas, galleries, verandas or just plain porches, will be seen to play an important part in the outside appearance of the houses. And if they don't happen to appear in the pictures, it is because, as Mr. Attmore says, they are "sometime back of the house." They derive from a design idea commonly supposed to have been imported from the British West Indies, where porches and galleries had earlier been widely developed by English settlers as protection from the even greater "Summer Heats" in those islands. And it is true that in the days of trade by sailing vessels there was many a close connection between the West Indies and almost all the Carolina coastal towns, New Bern included. But the colonial archi-

tecture of places like the Bahamas had far less influence on the houses of New Bern than it had a little farther south, as for instance on the houses of Charleston. The influence that New Bern felt most, and the one that immediately strikes the student of early American homebuilding trends when he sees the old New Bern houses, was the influence of New England; and particularly are there striking similarities between certain of the houses here and houses in Farmington, Connecticut, and Salem, Massachusetts. And there is a ready explanation for this, too. For there was constant coming and going by sea, to and from ports of call in Massachusetts and Connecticut. Carpenters and other craftsmen, having freshly finished a house or two in Farmington, say, would turn up in New Bern, and take on a house or two here. These men might even have stopped over in the West Indies on the way, for the trading voyages were often made in this triangular fashion. In this way, did ideas in house design travel and take root.

How so many of the fine New Bern houses managed to survive is a matter that also can be pieced together after a fashion. One thing that has happened elsewhere, and that

*The Smallwood-Ward House, in New Bern: 1812*

Right now it is even more of a rarity, for among the surviving great country houses of the region none has been restored with greater skill, taste and largess. It was in 1810, on Edisto Island, about thirty miles below Charleston, that a man named William Seabrook, with a fortune from sea-island cotton burning a hole in his pocket, built this beauty of an Adamesque mansion. The house is as hard to come upon by road today as is many a fine old tidewater establishment in Maryland or Virginia (and as rewarding when you do); the reason being that most of them originally were built to be reached mainly by sailing boat—just as Seabrook, as elsewhere noted, was reached one day when it was new by Lafayette, coming over from Charleston to call.

happened here, was what occurred in the change-over from trade and travel by sea to trade and travel by land. The busier routes of commerce began to run in other directions, and New Bern no longer lay in a position where the pace of progress was as ruthless in respect to pleasant antiquities as is often the case. Another thing was that during the Civil War, when many engaging southern towns were being damaged or destroyed by various acts of violence, New Bern was occupied by Federal troops, and thus was being in a sense protected and preserved. As a matter of fact, it was the Taylor-Ward house here that served as the 45th Massachusetts Regimental Headquarters, and it is apparent that it was treated with unusual respect. Then New Bern had also been fortunate as to fire. It is true that in 1798 an extraordinary structure known as Tryon's Palace, which was General Assembly hall, capital offices and Governor's residence combined, was destroyed by fire that started when a Negro woman with a torch was searching in the cellar for eggs. But in 1922, when a three-day, forty-block fire was raging, the fine old residential district was saved by a shift of the wind. And thus do certain historical attractions remain as others disappear.

Plans are under way for the restoration of Tryon's Palace, and when this has been accomplished, it will be a further incentive to the fine old houses of the town to stay as fine as they are, of which the two depicted here are outstanding examples.

IN the days down here when cotton, rice and indigo were creating Carolina wealth, Seabrook was considered one of the handsomest of Low Country plantation houses.

IN the two New Bern houses shown here, which can hold their own with the finest, the emphasis is on livability rather than impressiveness. Early New Bernians appreciated quality and beautiful workmanship but had little desire for magnificence. In the downstairs drawing room of the Taylor-Ward house (next page) on Craven Street the arched reveals are typical of several houses in the town. In the Smallwood-Ward dining room (page 121) you see them again flanking the door that leads into the hall.

The carving in both houses is very fine, indeed. Note that the paneled dado with its rope-molding finish runs right around the alcoves of the Smallwood-Ward dining room. The mahogany Chippendale furniture might almost be said to be part of the color scheme, so much glow and richness does it add to the room.

The dining room opens into the living room (page 121), whose woodwork is of a piece with the dining room. Anyone familiar with the Salem woodwork in the early

*Seabrook Plantation, on Edisto Island, South Carolina: 1810*

*The Taylor-Ward Drawing Room*

In the drawing room and master bedroom of the Taylor-Ward house, the detail in mantels and door frames is notable for its Colonial dignity. Placed on either side of the fireplace, here, is a charming pair of Victorian tufted chairs, which with the heirloom brasses, the Turkish carpet and the many fine engravings, give this room a delightful air of warm and hospitable living. The bedroom, seen through the piers of the great four-poster, was originally the upstairs drawing room.

*A Bedroom in the Taylor-Ward House*

The Victorian décor here is quite typical of New Bern drawing rooms, where the furnishings are usually family possessions.

The dining room in the Smallwood-Ward house is designed to bring out all of the beauty of the woodwork and the alcoves, the wallpaper panels adding richness to the scheme. The feature of the room, of course, is the matching tripod tables in the alcoves with identical mirrors over them and identical candelabra and urns on them.

*The Smallwood-Ward Living Room*

*The Smallwood-Ward Dining Room*

*The Stair Hall at Seabrook*

1800's will note a similarity in the carving, especially in the ceiling cornices.

SEABROOK PLANTATION. Not the least of the wonders in this fabulous plantation home is the double staircase, sweeping gracefully through the great framing archway to join at the landing and ascend to a wide hallway above. Untold yards of hard-to-find ingrain carpeting, a tapestry-like weave of almost a century ago, cover the whole hall and the staircases, which bracket a view across terraces, gardens and pools to the tidewater estuary upon which this great estate is so peacefully and appropriately situated.

The drawing room is pure Adamesque perfection,

which was the fashion of Federal times when the Seabrook house was built. The present owners are not afraid of color; their bold and skillful use of it brings their old house vividly alive.

The dining room is dominated by the immense triple doors with their glazed flat arch, through which you can see the identical doorway opposite, opening into the drawing room shown here. The drape paper, in tones of deep gold and lavender, is of just the right redness for this room. The floral carpet is more of the ingrain variety. The engraving between the long windows is of Lafayette, a personal friend of the builder, who visited here (arriving by water from Charleston), and stood as godfather to one of the Seabrook children.

*The Seabrook Dining Room*

*The Seabrook Drawing Room*
*Color picks out the exquisite detail of the carved woodwork and fine paneling. It is used again in a subtle blending of patterns in wallpaper and satin upholstery, their delicacy accentuated by the firmer accents of draperies and hearth rug. The portrait over the mantel is of the owner's great-grandmother, Elizabeth Thompson Dodge of Annapolis, Maryland.*

*The Nathaniel Russell House: 1807*

*The Young-Johnson House: 1770*

## Upstairs and Down in Charleston

MANY people every spring find old Charleston streets irresistible. The color scheme is of a kind you seldom encounter—a medley of whites, pinks, yellows, pale greens, blues, and even purples—just considering the houses, and not even counting the colors rampant in the gardens and all around the sidewalk vendors. Add to this medley of color another medley,

of the picturesque and the stately, and you can't help thinking what a sight it is to see. But it is indoors that Charleston approaches pure perfection; and of all indoors, in her drawing rooms. This could easily be because Charleston has been from the beginning the most sociable of cities. In each elegant old house there are as a rule two separate drawing rooms: one upstairs, one down.

*The John Stuart House: 1772*

*The Brandford-Horry House: 1751*

The one upstairs was generally the more formal, with the finer woodwork, the choicer furnishings. It was the one from which the hostess said good-by to her departing guests, the host taking leave of them downstairs at the door. The graciousness of these drawing rooms goes well with people. And the beauty of the houses harmonizes with the behavior of everybody about them.

STUART. The upstairs drawing room in the Georgian house that Colonel John Stuart built on Tradd Street represents most faithfully its original character and quality. For everything you see here of the room itself—the paneling, the overmantel, the pedimented doorways, fireplace and plasterwork, is the remarkable reproduction of the original shell, now assembled in the Kansas City Art Museum; the room now being literally in two places at once. Here where it belongs, it is beautifully furnished for living, with a flavor that reflects the whole fine eighteenth-century spirit of the room as it existed before.

RUSSELL. So far as we know this is the first public appearance in print of the Nathaniel Russell house interiors. Nor have these rooms ever been open to the public. So this constitutes a kind of debut for one of the outstanding examples of Adam décor in this country. The first-floor drawing room, page 126, is the formal receiving room, its decoration here of an almost classic formality. The delicate tones of walls and carpet create a subdued, crepuscular light in these rooms whose curving lines give emphasis to their tranquillity. Over the living room mantel is an unsigned Dutch floral painting, the bouquet on the table repeating it in a riot of roses, lilies and tulips. The crocus bowls set on the mantel beneath are rare Pinxton.

Upstairs the sitting room (page 126) is more ornate and much less formal. The cornices over the windows, the deep ceiling cornice, all are encrusted with delicate Adam ornamentation that is reminiscent of the jeweler's art. The glass chandeliers are as fine as the woodwork.

*The Stuart Upstairs Drawing Room*

*The Nathaniel Russell Upstairs Drawing Room
This room is furnished predominantly
for comfortable living; some quite modern
pieces mixed in with rarities, such as the
tiny, spindly splay-legged table next to a
Queen Anne upholstered armchair over by
the fireplace. Crown Derby graces the
mantel along with a modern timepiece.*

*The Nathaniel Russell Downstairs Drawing Room
The beautiful eighteenth-century Chippendale mirror, repeated on the other side of
the doorway, leads into a hall whose
glories you can only glimpse. The staircase, which literally floats in the air, is
a piece of architectural pyrotechnics, a
tour de force of the joiner's skill.*

*The Brandford-Horry Upstairs Drawing Room*
*Without exaggeration the wall shown here, if*
*not the purest architecturally, may be said*
*to be one of the most beautiful in America.*

*The Brandford-Horry Downstairs Drawing Room*
*The delft tiles facing the fireplace, the muted*
*brilliance of the Chinese rug, the openness of*
*the shield-back Hepplewhite settee and chairs*
*add to the lightness and sparkle.*

127

*The Young-Johnson Upstairs Drawing Room*

BRANDFORD-HORRY. As you enter, you are struck by the brightness and lightness of the drawing room (page 127), whose beautiful, quite simple paneling is a background for a dazzling display of antique china ornaments, of which the owner has a notable collection. The many little figurines, the vases, jars, lamps, and tea service, everything is discreetly placed where it suits the room best, with the collector's skill for advantageous arrangement.

Upstairs, in marked contrast, is the living room (page 127) with its dark, natural-wood paneling. Only recently has it been restored to its original state, the unusual beauty of the native cypress brought out by long hand-rubbing. The darker woods in the carved pilasters, cornices and ornamentation are tulip and mahogany. Again you can see more amazing china on mantel, bureau and tables.

YOUNG-JOHNSON. This small and early house is owned by a sculptor of note, with a talent for collecting. Wilmer Hoffman has made of his house not only a bewitching informal home, but a place where every wall and corner contains something rare and exciting to look at. In this brilliant upstairs drawing room which you see above, the portrait of the delicate, rosy boy hanging above the mantelpiece draws you to it like a magnet. It is a portrait of Mr. Hoffman's uncle, as a child, whom Thomas Sully chose to paint wearing the same dilapidated straw hat in which he had posed his own son for the famous portrait now in Boston. Sully grew up in Charleston and did much of his best work here; his total production is said to have been 2600 paintings.

Among other minor masterpieces in Mr. Hoffman's collection are paintings by Goya, Sir Thomas Lawrence, and a second Sully. Since Mr. Hoffman has traveled much, heirlooms are the background here for fascinating *objets d'arts* from all over the world. He has allowed a very few of his own fine pieces of sculpture modest places in the house. What the house lacks in size, it more than makes up for in style.

# On Savannah Squares

THE WINBURN HOUSE AND

THE ANDERSON HOUSE

*The Winburn House: Early Nineteenth Century*

THE finest of the houses that line Savannah streets and frame her fascinating squares range from Adamesque through Regency into Classic and Gothic revivals. But more than a study in styles, it is the present romantic appearance of the Savannah houses in their settings which gives the city its peculiar appeal. And it is the squares that are especially pictorial. Generally with a monument or fountain half hidden in the middle among live oaks and palmettos, the surrounding façades form a frieze of soft yellows, pinks and chalky whites, marked off with ornamental ironwork and held together by garden walls crowded over with crape myrtle and glossy green magnolias.

It is this scheme of squares that makes Savannah unique among American cities; somewhat reminiscent of the French city of Nancy. The plan was based on a sketch in *Villas of the Ancients* by Robert Castell, who died in a debtors' prison in England, a horror which the state of Georgia was founded expressly to alleviate.

WINBURN HOUSE. Here, as in most finely furnished homes in Savannah, Empire predominates, being part and parcel of the period. From the airy and atmospheric dining and drawing rooms, here the deep bay windows face out upon one of the many flowery squares of Savannah. Through the window you may catch glimpses of the wrought-iron balconies with which this house like so many others in the city is festooned. Hepplewhite, Sheraton and Duncan Phyfe complement the Empire pieces.

These rooms are a reflection of the colorful streets and squares on which the houses stand. The tall, wide openings of windows and doors, the height of the ceilings, and the way the architecture is detailed and decorated recall

*The Square of the Anderson House: Early Nineteenth Century*

*The Winburn Dining and Drawing Rooms*

the generally square block forms of the houses as seen from without—wide and high, and decorated with arabesques of ironwork and with simple, sober Empire ornament. It is a pleasant repetition of a certain effect, inside and out, that helps to establish more vividly the Savannah character.

ANDERSON HOUSE. With what clarity do some houses describe the people who live in them. The Anderson house is such a house—not only beautiful in itself, but beautiful because a family has occupied it gently for generations, cherishing it and one another. Births, marriages and deaths all form a part of its history, as with every house, but here it is written plain for the discerning eye that they took their natural course in an harmonious community of feeling.

Cornices, ceiling medallions, doorway details, marble mantels, all belong to the rich decorative period that produced the furniture, as well as the gaslight chandelier. The colors are warm and spicy, and yet the house is so well ordered that the impression is one of cool tranquillity. In the dining room the door frames, so typical of the Napoleonic influence in the Greek Revival, are painted black, strikingly emphasizing their character. Much of the furniture here is Empire, and the portraits, many of which are family, add to the glowing impression.

In the lofty-ceilinged drawing room, the graceful Empire chaise sets the tone. But the most important piece here is the cane-seated open armchair with its back to you, which belonged to Thomas Jefferson. The ornaments, mirrors, lamps and clocks are simply the charmingly chosen accessories of generations of people of taste. If ever it might be said that a house had a kind of radiance about it, it would be this one.

*The Anderson Living Room*

*The Anderson Dining Room*

*Andrew Jackson's Bedroom*

# The Splendor of Tennessee

## THE HERMITAGE AND BELLE MEADE, NASHVILLE

THE first President to make a point of plainness was in the White House when a courier from Nashville brought word in 1831 that the Hermitage had been gutted by fire. The big brick mansion had been built by the hero of New Orleans about a dozen years before, from all accounts an edifice of considerable plainness itself. But its blackened walls still stood up so strong that word went back to start from there rebuilding right away.

In view of Jackson's disapproval of pomp, the only explanation for the great Corinthian portico that eventually appeared across the front of the Hermitage as part of the restoration, was a romantic rage for the classical look in architecture, then at such a fever pitch that even the humblest dwellings were being built to resemble little Greek temples. Now, after a century or more, the columns, the gaudy carpeting, the tassels, are all part of the Hermitage's period charm, making a most personal and moving monument to one of our greatest Americans.

It was about 1825 that wealthy Tennessee planters began to feel they needed something more impressive, less restrained, than the refinements of Adamesque and the earlier Colonial styles in which their houses up to then had been built in memory of Maryland, Virginia and the Carolinas, from where these men had emigrated. And as it happened, there were carpenter-contractors working their way West from the seaboard states, who were able to satisfy the grandiloquent requirements of the plantation proprietors. They brought with them as entourage their families and their slaves. On their way West they stopped to build houses for anybody able to pay; making the bricks themselves from the nearest claybank, taking the timber themselves from the trees.

It was one such enterprising outfit, headed by two men named Joseph Rieff and William C. Hume, which arrived around Nashville just in time to rebuild the Hermitage for the President. And the house as you see it here was their handiwork.

*The Hermitage, near Nashville: 1831*

By the middle of the century, the rich agricultural lands of central Tennessee were piling up such fortunes for their proprietors that it was only natural that these gentlemen should strive to outdo one another in the grandeur of their mansions. Built on a palatial scale, with dramatic disregard for cost, and furnished in keeping, the three houses generally acknowledged to have come out on top were Belle Meade and Belmont at Nashville, and a monumental residence of the Polk family, some forty miles to the south, which having changed hands in a dice game was called Rattle and Snap—a house as extraordinary as its name, with ten Corinthian columns two stories tall, two spiral staircases, a great double dining room for banquets, and a ballroom of regimental proportions. Even so, Belmont, which is now a school for girls, was probably the most ornate of the three, and Belle Meade the most spectacular, the work of the distinguished Philadelphia architect, William Strickland, who had come out to design his famous capitol building at Nashville.

Belle Meade was built for a General William Giles Harding who was born in a log cabin on the west side of the present front lawn—such were the rises in fortunes in the Tennessee of that era. The property took in 5,300 acres, and the General turned it into what became the greatest stud farm of its day. The mansion, with its deer park and its peacocks, was the show place of the state. And just as it rose then to outrival all the other great houses of the region, it has now outlived all but a few of its past competitors, most of them fading memories of bygone splendor.

THE HERMITAGE. All of the furniture in the front parlor and the back parlor belonged to Jackson, and belonged just where you see it in these rooms today. It is as though time had stood still. The lovely crystal chandelier, the Japanese bronze clock inlaid with enamel, the Dresden vases, the brass lamps with crystal prisms, the silver filigree basket holding the roses, and in the farther parlor Mrs. Jackson's guitar and her sewing box inlaid with mother-of-pearl, (its faded spools of silk still inside), the pair of silver luster vases sent by the Czar of Russia— all these and much, much more were part of the paraphernalia of daily life of a great and honored man. The heavy damask draperies, the richly patterned Victorian carpet, probably woven in France, velvet divans and carved chairs, all breathe not only of the Victorian in-

*The Hermitage Parlors*

*Belle Meade, at Nashville: Early Nineteenth Century*

fluence in furniture, but also of the General and President himself, whose powerful personality left its stamp on his home as well as on his country.

His bedroom (page 133) is just as it was the day he died there in 1845. Here are his leather hat-box for his tall beaver, his tobacco box, the portraits of his family, the prints of battle scenes, his wash-stand and the mirror where he shaved, his chair near the fireside. Even the wallpaper has not been changed. The handmade bedspread has his initials "A.J." embroidered on it by some loving and familiar hand.

BELLE MEADE. A Victorian period piece at its most lush. The uncrowded spaces (page 136) can take the plush, the gilt and the carving in their stride. So vast is the scale that the two grand pianos are easily absorbed in it. Look well at the intricately carved Belter chairs standing at either end of the twin fireplaces, for they represent the apex

of a type of cabinet work now extinct. All of the furniture is of carved mahogany and rosewood. Carved are the regal gilt cornices over the draperies and the huge gilt mirrors.

The hallway, fourteen feet wide and forty-two feet long, with its red velours carpet and graceful staircase, made an enchanting setting for the reception of brilliant gatherings when the era of opulent Southern hospitality was at its height. The scale is carried out here in wallpaper pattern, vases, and even in the broad stripe of the upholstery on the Empire couch; for anything dainty would be dwarfed. When you climb the stairs and look down, you get to know what a massive house you are in.

Upstairs, a glance at the double bedroom may lead you to think the effect is achieved with mirrors. But not so. The two manorial beds are really there, each with its regal tester, so high that no breeze will ever be shut out on a warm summer night. In these twin rooms almost all the furniture is identical.

*The Belle Meade Salon*

*The Belle Meade Hallway*

*Two Belle Meade Bedrooms*

# HOW WE FOUND THE HOUSES

## A NOTE BY DOROTHY PRATT

HOUSES, like people, can be very beautiful and still not be photogenic. This is only one of the reasons why it has taken a lot of searching to locate the houses in this book. The houses were selected, paradoxically, to please the widest possible audience as well as the limited one of connoisseurs. Their likings are not so far apart as you might think. Thus the houses must be not only distinguished architecturally but also representative of their type, so that the reader may see how the best houses looked which were building at that particular time and in that particular place. In addition they must have been tenderly and skillfully treated by their owners so as to preserve and enhance all their good points. Finally, the furnishings had to be in keeping with the house. This takes only a minute to say, but for a house to meet these specifications fully is another matter. Sometimes in certain sections of the country it has taken years to find just what we were looking for. And sometimes we have made three or four separate trips to a single area, with nothing to show for it all in the end.

In the beginning ten years ago, when the regional project started, we telescoped the whole procedure into single trips for which we made no advance preparations. We were feeling our way. And of course before the articles had begun to appear, we had nothing to show. We were prepared to be away three or four weeks at a time, for it took that long to find the houses, send for the photographers, and then do the photographing. When we could not discover a person who could and would break the ice for us with the home owners, we simply rang doorbells, knowing that we might be turned down before we entered the house. This part of the job usually fell to me since my husband always managed to be very busy with his big camera when there was doorbell ringing to do. That was the way we got permission to photograph one of the greatest houses in this country; with me standing at the door for twenty minutes waiting for the owner, far off within the wonderful old house, to make up his mind to see me.

Once the permission was given to photograph, there remained the question of whether the owner would be ready for "the ordeal by photography" in a matter of two or three days. Next . . . how soon could the photographer manage to get there? Many other arrangements had to be made. Sometimes in cities, such as Charleston and Savannah, the police department had to be asked to keep the street in front of the houses clear of cars when we were doing the exteriors. Sometimes electric current was inadequate and generator trucks had to be hired. Always there were flowers to be arranged which would suit each house.

But after we had been at it for a while, we worked out a less difficult system. It takes longer, perhaps, but in the end has proven kinder to us and to the home owners. Now we make two trips, one to look and one to photograph. Besides saving wear on all concerned, there is something good about letting your impressions sink in and ferment for a time, before coming to a decision. For after you have looked at ten to twenty-five houses in a day or so, you can go pretty blank on the whole thing; just as you do in an art gallery when you have had a surfeit of pictures, no matter how fine they are. As a rule the judgment is better when a little time has elapsed. Of course this is not always true either. For quite often one or both of us will exclaim in two minutes after entering a house, "This is it." When it comes over you like that, you don't have to worry any more—unless you still have to ask the owner if she or he is willing.

One other question that should not be overlooked, and which is specifically covered by the acknowledgments that follow, is the matter of help in finding the houses. The study of books naturally leads to the right localities, but without a key person in each area (someone who has been *inside* the houses) the search could be endless and perhaps fruitless as well. Finding the person happens in many different ways and sometimes so oddly that it almost seems as though a certain magic were operating in our favor.

So it turns out that this book is not only a collaboration between the Pratts, but a collaboration in which many other people play a very important part, and without whom the making of the book would hardly have been possible.

# THE PHOTOGRAPHERS AND THE
# PHOTOGRAPHING

## ANOTHER NOTE BY DOROTHY PRATT

I WISH I had kept count of the number of people who have said to me, "What fun your work must be." The inflection is always one that seems to add, "If you could *call* it work." Actually I guess it is about the hardest work I have ever done. The photographers work three times as hard, but never tell you so. Their equipment weighs a ton and it is like unpacking a circus to get it in and out of a house. Then there is inevitably a lot of furniture to be moved to bring the most interesting pieces into the picture, which unfortunately can only take in part of a room. Sometimes there are large rugs to be laid or moved from room to room, large pictures to be rehung. And all the while a big battery of powerful lights is creating a torrid temperature; which, of course, has its advantages only in cold weather and when you are photographing an unheated house.

My part of the photographing is to "set up" the pictures, or at any rate to say what I think should be left in or taken out, and to arrange the bouquets. The photographer usually tells me after the bouquet is confected that it is either too high or too low or too thin or too fat, so that I have to pull it apart and start all over. Actually he could arrange the flowers much better than I do, but he has matters of greater moment on his mind. Once in a while Ezra Stoller and I have big fights about what should or should not be in a picture, and he says that I always win; but that is just the smoke screen in back of which he does as he thinks best.

Sometimes the owners or custodians of the houses we picture cannot see why we must move things around, and some even feel the room won't be recognizable. But in all of the houses so far, not a single person whose house is in this book has continued to feel that way after seeing the finished picture.

Our endeavor is to bring out the best and most interesting points, both in the architecture and decoration of each room; and in order to do that in a limited space, it necessarily takes a good deal of arranging, or what we like to call composing. We hope to convey the feeling of each room, the feeling that it gives you when you actually walk into it and look around. And in addition to all this, we want to make beautiful pictures that will cause readers to exclaim with delight when they look at them.

There is only one more thing to add, and that is about the people who own the houses and who are kind enough to allow them to be pictured in this way for the public. I think they deserve some kind of medal for all their trouble, their patience and particularly for their generosity in making their intimate treasures available to us and to you.

AS the pictures are the most important part of this book, it seemed to us that the reader should have a chance to hear directly from at least one of the photographers. And as it happens that in this volume of the *Treasury*, Ezra Stoller has taken a large majority of the interiors, it has fallen to him to give his version of what the work was like. Each of the three men involved in the major photographing for this book works in his own way his wonders to perform. Each one for his photographs here chose to use a Deardorff 8x10 view camera, and each one used Goerz Dagor lenses, from wide-angle to 14-inch focal length. From there on, each one had his own techniques, his own particular types of lighting equipment, his own pet ways of operating.

Ezra Stoller has made architectural photography a specialty, and in that particular field he has no peer. Wesley Balz is the well-known photographic illustrator, who takes on any sort of assignment with complete aplomb. Harold Fowler, a pioneer in color photography, has been photographing *Ladies' Home Journal* decorating and food pages since 1933.

*Ladies and gentlemen, Mr. Stoller:*

"Until asked by Richard Pratt to photograph for the Regional Series in the *Ladies' Home Journal*, I had scarcely ever been in a fine traditional house. As far as I was concerned, anything built before 1900 was in a class with the pyramids; interesting, but mostly for the archeologist. It was a surprise to me, and I think a matter of more than casual interest, that Mr. Pratt decided to work with someone who had not only been trained in modern architecture but had established his reputation as a photographer of modern architecture entirely.

"What an awakening it was, and how much I have learned by my association with these great old houses, can hardly be described. No longer am I able to look at a "modern" house with the same undiluted enthusiasm. I can see now that the consciousness of the composition of spaces and their use, which is what all true architecture is about, is no more acute now than it was when these early homes were built. In short, since good taste is timeless, perhaps Mr. Pratt felt that these great houses of their day ought to be pictured by a person trained to see the finest in contemporary architecture.

"It is noteworthy that the technique entailed in photographing these old houses is so much different from that applied in documenting most contemporary homes. Both pattern and texture play a more important part, especially in the fine handcrafted woodwork and furniture. The materials are richer and the use of color generally more subtle. Because it had not the freedom of fenestration allowed by modern building methods and materials, and because the way of life oriented the house inward as a frame for a more formal life, the quality of the light in the eighteenth-century house is far different from that of today. This last is most important since it is the prime factor in establishing the mood of a room, and a photographer must take the existing light as a theme for whatever he adds.

"The rigid limitations of modern color film make it almost impossible to use the existing light alone and it often takes much ingenuity to work with it rather than to superimpose a pattern of our own. Then, too, the electrical wiring in these houses was generally installed many years ago and was rarely able to cope with the load we would have put upon it. Hence an almost complete electrical system had to be part of our equipment. How well I re-member Dr. and Mrs. Andrews' little Shaker house, and my feelings as we were unloading our many hundreds of pounds of lighting equipment, upon being told that the closest electricity was at the pole line half a mile down the road. We had to shoot this house with flash.

"Since we were rarely able to anticipate what film would be required, we had to load our film holders on the job, and darkrooms were improvised in most fantastic places. My long-suffering assistant still breaks into a sweat and suffers a cramp as he looks at one of these photographs and recalls the airless tiny closets in which he has spent so much time.

"The economy of magazine space being what it is, we were often forced to convey the spirit of a house in but three or four pictures. This entailed great selectivity and usually a good deal of rearranging and furniture moving— more aches for myself and assistant. Under Mrs. Pratt's discerning and relentless eye no detail was too small nor highboy too heavy to require our attention and only occasionally was it in exactly the right spot; even when it was, the rug would have to be moved, so we were trapped anyhow. Without Mrs. Pratt's instinct for the appropriate and beautiful, little of the warmth and livability of these interiors would have manifested itself. There's no question but that if we had to photograph a bare tent in the middle of the Sahara, she would produce an exquisite prayer rug and a fabulous coffee service, before we would set up our camera.

"Not the least of a photographer's problems concern themselves with soothing the anxieties of the homeowners who are subjected to his camera. Here these good people have given so much of themselves to restoring and furnishing these old houses only to be descended upon by a horde of people with great disreputable cases of ominous gear. What restraint and patience they must have exercised in their anxiety. How could they ever believe that no damage would be done and that their houses would be left as we had found them? For this, the sight of the architectural editor hovering about seemed to be all the reassurance they required."

# ACKNOWLEDGMENTS

These people, and these organizations, by their helpfulness in all sorts of ways, and by their participation, active and passive, have contributed mightily to the completion of this whole presentation.

### Maine

Mr. and Mrs. Edward Browning of the Ruggles House Society and Mary Ruggles Chandler of the Ruggles house.

Mr. and Mrs. Donald D. Dodge of Spite House.

For the Tate house, Mrs. Clinton W. Davis and the National Society of Colonial Dames in Maine.

For the Lady Pepperrell mansion, Miss Rosamund Thaxter, Miss Dorothy Vaughan, Mr. Douglas Armsden and the Society for the Preservation of New England Antiquities.

All Maine photographs by Ezra Stoller, except Douglas Armsden's exterior of the Lady Pepperrell mansion.

### New Hampshire

Mr. Ralph May of the Rundlet-May house, and Mr. Bertram K. Little. Photographs by Ezra Stoller.

### Massachusetts

Dr. and Mrs. Edward D. Andrews of the Shaker house.

Mr. and Mrs. Henry R. Atkinson of the Old Heath house.

Mrs. F. Gordon Patterson of the Gore Place Society.

Mr. and Mrs. Robert W. Atkins of East Brick.

Mr. and Mrs. Burnam Dell of the Dell house.

Mr. and Mrs. Bertram K. Little of Cogswell's Grant, with a special bow to the helpfulness of Mrs. Little's expert knowledge on many occasions, and to Mr. Little's, too, as director of the Society for the Preservation of New England Antiquities.

All photographs of Massachusetts houses above by Ezra Stoller.

Mrs. Gretchen Girdler of the Lee mansion and the Marblehead Historical Society. Photographs by Harold Fowler.

### Rhode Island

Mrs. Antoinette F. Downing for widespread help and expert advice.

Mr. John Nicholas Brown of the Nightingale-Brown house.

Rhode Island School of Design, owners of the Carrington house.

Mrs. Robert P. Brown of the Eliza Ward house.

Photographs by Ezra Stoller.

### Connecticut

Mrs. Frank Cogan, secretary of the Antiquarian and Landmarks Society, Inc., of Connecticut, for widespread helpfulness.

Mrs. William E. Parsons and the Connecticut Society of the Colonial Dames of America for the Webb house.

Mrs. Cogan for the Hale house.

Mr. and Mrs. Henry M. Clark for Hastings Hill.

Mr. and Mrs. Wilmarth Lewis for the Solomon Cowles house.

Mrs. H. W. Sage for the George Cowles house.

Mr. and Mrs. Heinz Warneke for The Mowings.

Mr. Frédèric Palmer for Dunstaffnage.

Mr. and Mrs. Robert I. Carter for the Lord house.

Mr. Williams Haynes and the Denison Society for the Denison house.

Mr. and Mrs. Stephen Hurlbutt for Anguilla.

Mr. and Mrs. Haynes for Stonecrop.

All Connecticut photographs by Ezra Stoller, except The Mowings, Dunstaffnage and the Lord house, which are by Harold Fowler.

### New York

Mr. James M. Leith and the Columbia County Historical Society for the House of History.

Mr. and Mrs. Herman S. Murray and the Town of Hempstead for Rock Hall.

The Village of East Hampton for Home Sweet Home.

Photographs by Ezra Stoller, except exterior of House of History, by Wayne Andrews.

### Pennsylvania

Mrs. James I. Wendell and the Pennsylvania Historical and Museum Commission for Pottsgrove.

Captain Edmund A. Crenshaw, Jr., and the Morris House Committee of the Germantown Historical Society for the Morris house.

Photographs by Ezra Stoller.

The Commonwealth of Pennsylvania for Washington's Valley Forge Headquarters.

Headquarters photographs by Wesley Balz.

## Delaware

Mr. Donald V. L. Downs for Aspendale.
Mrs. Henry Ridgely for the House on the Green.
Photographs by Ezra Stoller.

## Maryland

Mrs. H. Rowland Clapp, Mrs. Blanchard Randall and the Maryland House and Garden Pilgrimage Committee for over-all helpfulness.
The Misses Davidson and Mr. Stuart Davidson for Cremona.
Cremona photographs by Wesley Balz.
Mr. and Mrs. Lewis R. Andrews for Tulip Hill.
Mr. and Mrs. Frederick C. Thomas for Troth's Fortune.
Mr. and Mrs. Charles Lipscomb for Boston Cliff.
Photographs by Ezra Stoller.

## District of Columbia

Mr. and Mrs. George M. Morris for The Lindens.
Mrs. R. M. Templeman and the National Society of the Colonial Dames in the District of Columbia for Dumbarton House.
Photographs by Ezra Stoller.

## Virginia

Mrs. Herbert Claiborne and the Colonial Dames of America in the State of Virginia for Wilton, and Mrs. Claiborne for much over-all helpfulness.
Mrs. H. H. Smith and the Kenmore Association, Inc., for Kenmore.
Colonial Williamsburg, Inc., for the Brush-Everard house, and Mr. Laurence Kocher and Mr. Robert Hoke for over-all helpfulness.

Mr. James Cogar for the Nicolson house.
The National Park Service for the Moore house.
Photographs by Wesley Balz.

## The Carolinas

Mr. and Mrs. David L. Ward for the Taylor-Ward house.
Mr. and Mrs. William Ward for the Smallwood-Ward house.
Mrs. Bess Hyman Guion for great helpfulness.
Mr. and Mrs. Donald D. Dodge for Seabrook Plantation.
Mr. and Mrs. Jack Wing for the John Stuart house.
Mr. and Mrs. Percy Kammerer for the Brandford-Horry house.
The late Mrs. Francis Joseph Pelzer for the Nathaniel Russell house.
Mr. Wilmer Hoffman for the Young-Johnson house.
Mrs. S. Henry Edmunds for over-all helpfulness.
The New Bern photographs by Wesley Balz; all others in the Carolinas by Ezra Stoller.

## Georgia

Mr. and Mrs. W. A. Winburn for the Winburn house.
Mrs. J. Randolph Anderson and the late Mr. Anderson for the Anderson house.
Mr. and Mrs. Buford Smith for over-all helpfulness.
Photographs by Ezra Stoller.

## Tennessee

The Society for the Preservation of Tennessee Antiquities for Belle Meade.
The Ladies Hermitage Association for the Hermitage.
Photographs by Ezra Stoller.

# INDEX

# The Authors and Their Book

RICHARD PRATT, architectural editor of the Ladies' Home Journal, was born in Steelton, Pennsylvania, in 1891. Educated in the public schools of Steelton and Harrisburg, he taught himself architecture and landscaping. He practiced landscape architecture in Baltimore and, while there, began to write for House and Garden and the Baltimore News, for which he was art and music critic. His work in Baltimore was interrupted by eighteen months' overseas service in France with the U. S. Army during World War I; two years after his return, he left to become managing editor of House and Garden. Later, he was appointed editor of The Seven Seas. He joined the Ladies' Home Journal in 1936. His first book was *The Picture Garden Book* (Howell, Soskin, 1942), illustrated with color photographs by Edward Steichen. This was followed by *A Treasury of Early American Homes* (Whittlesey House, 1949), which has sold more than 250,000 copies. In 1927, Mr. Pratt married his present collaborator, Dorothy Michaels Pratt, who works with him on all his projects but who has not been given public credit for her extensive collaboration until the publication of this book. Since their marriage, the Pratts have lived on a farm in Bucks County, Pennsylvania, which is devoted to the practical working out of experiments in architectural and landscape design. They are now at work on a comprehensive guide to early American homes, a garden book and a book on modern houses.

THE SECOND TREASURY OF EARLY AMERICAN HOMES (Hawthorn Books, 1954) was designed and its production supervised by Abe Lerner and George Hornby. It was set on the Monotype by The Curtis Publishing Company in Baskerville, a modernized reproduction of the types cut in 1760 by John Baskerville of Birmingham, England, who was first a writing master and later became one of England's greatest printers. Most of the color engravings were made by the Beck Engraving Company. The book was printed by the American Colortype Company at Allwood, Clifton, New Jersey, on Warren's Lustro Gloss, a clay-coated paper manufactured by the S. D. Warren Company. The binding was done by American Book-Stratford Press, Inc., in New York City.

A HAWTHORN BOOK